The Game of Truth

A Humorous Guide to Self-Discovery

Francisco Bontempi, M.D.
Fernando Bontempi

In collaboration with Annette Segal

Illustrated by Sendra

Educational
DYNAMICS PRESS

1010 University Avenue #427
San Diego, CA 92103
www.gameoftruth.com

What People Are Saying About The Game of Truth

If you like intimate sharing among friends, here is something that you will surely enjoy; if, on the other hand, you feel that some excitement is missing in your reunions, here is something that may be of help.

Dr. Claudio Naranjo MD, Author
The End of Patriarchy

Wow! A powerful tool that helped me see who my friends really are!

Gail Feinstein-Forman, Author
Burning Beds and Mermaids

"This is a wonderful book and a must read!"

Eric Jensen, Author
The Learning Brain

ISBN # 0-9668876-0-3
Library of Congress Catalog Card Number 99-72266

HOW TO ORDER
By Fax: (619) 542-1612
By Mail: Educational Dynamics Press
1010 University Avenue #427
San Diego, CA 92103
educdynam@aol.com
www.gameoftruth.com
1-800-888-4741

Editor's Acknowledgement

The voyage of discovery consists not in seeking new landscapes,
but in having new eyes.

~ Marcel Proust 1871-1922

Every project is a voyage of discovery. While navigating "the rapids" and when enjoying the beautiful "calms", people enrich, support and lend the hands that guide a creative effort to its ultimate destination. My love and thanks go out to the "hands" that guided this journey.

With deep love and eternal thanks to my friend, Julia, wherever she resides, for bequeathing me her wonderful brothers, Fernando and Francisco, who among their many gifts, brought "Truth" into my hands.

Hats off (my entire collection) in appreciation of the authors for their humor, intelligence and faith in my abilities to make their vision a reality.

A deep, rumbling laugh of appreciation for the brilliance of Sendra, who spiced the "Game" with his wonderful cartoons.

A bouquet of irises in gratitude and respect for the wonders of Bruce B. Brown who brought his aesthetic sensibilities to the layout of this project.

A deep curtsy in recognition of the joy and education that working with the amazing Jeffrey J. Strane and his team at Bay Port Press has wrought.

Yellow daisies to Ann Massey for her professionalism and cheer in the data entry department!

And finally, a treasured valentine to Scott Olesen for all the support, wisdom and balance he offered as the bill of fare on this journey!

Table of Contents

Image, Culture, & Ecology
History
The Game
How to Play

Author's Prologue

We used to sit in a circle. Boys and girls, aged 12, gathered together to play a game. We had no need for dice or a ball. It was an intense and passionate time that gave us a growing glimpse of ourselves and of the society in which we were evolving. We asked questions. We answered. This was the game of truth.

As the years went by, we each took different paths, one in psychiatry and alternative therapies, another in entrepreneurial adventures and so on. This, though, did not prevent us from getting together periodically to share one another's perceptions.

Children, nieces, nephews came into our lives. Once again we observed that ancient circle of boys and girls sitting on the floor and playing the game of truth – questioning themselves, laughing and feeling shame despite the laughter. The quest for truth appeared as vivid as before. Our adult eyes saw where we had been, what we had lived.

Friendships formed during childhood and adolescence have always been especially intense. At this age, one shares a certain degree of commitment that, in the complex and defensive/aggressive game of adults, is hidden under the subtle mechanisms of social roles.

In the adult world, true friendships are without doubt, a treasure. As adults, can we again play this somewhat faded game of truth from our past? Can we ask ourselves questions and be ready to expose our inner "I" truthfully to our friends and loved ones? Is it possible to find new and revitalizing relations through truth? Can we once again unearth the splendor of the childhood game?

And so the idea for this book came into being; a book around which to gather and face the eternal and ever present questions.

"Who am I?" Perhaps the most ancient question of all and probably at the root of our humanity. This question is one which we have all the time of our lives to answer, and the reflection of a group of friends to mine.

"Who am I?" When I think and speak about myself it is not my name that emerges from my conscience, but that monosyllabic grunt, that universal pronoun which we all call "I". No matter who we are, whether beggar or king, we all call ourselves by this international pronoun "I". Peter, Paul and Mary, Andrei, Indira, Françoise, Linpo, Aaron, Ali, Javier, N'ncomo, all call ourselves the same, "I". And what is the story behind this I, my story, your story?

In that old game of truth we found many answers. Beyond our personal name, we saw glimpses of essential similarities. What emerged from that common background, that profile of personal circumstances that the story of my friends allowed me to define? Who "I" am was in relation to others. When we were able to see how their answers uncovered their stories, how our answers portrayed ourselves, we could see that, despite each individual identity, the same "I" defined us all.

But the existence of truth without humor can be tragic. So many times we argued as children and even harder as adults for the sake of our personal truth:

> "But you told me..." "Liar!" "I told you the truth." "I always tell the truth!" "My beliefs are the right ones!" "Well, you're wrong!"

Is this not the foundation of much fighting and many wars? This is why in our approach to the existence of truth, humor is greatly needed – lots of it! In satisfying this need, we came across Sendra's wonderful illustrations for our project.

This book is intended for enjoyment, simply by leafing through it, or by a close reading, but most of all, by playing the game.

The freedom that inner truth can give us is a lot more fun than the serious-ness of our personal lies. The larger part of our habitual lies is unconscious. These lies are linked to our habits, becoming automatic and familiar. That is why as human beings, we are covered by an inseparable cloth of truth and lies.

So why don't YOU try – play to see how much of a mixture of truth and lies are in the story of your "I".

Many of the questions that are found in this book are taken from group therapy experiences. In these types of experiences it is not always easy to open up to others you don't know.

Quite often truth emerges as a progressive testing according to the quality of the group and each individual's intention. Of course, there are groups in which the laying bare of oneself would simply be stupid and inadvisable. We choose with whom we play. May your selection be wise and grant you happi-ness. But don't leave yourself out of the game. Sharing can be risky but the rewards are great.

Francisco Bontempi
Tegueste, Tenerife
1999

Purpose

"Know thyself," is the purpose of The Game of Truth. This book is for people dedicated to personal development. Through questions, interaction and humor, players discover more and more of themselves, their friends, family and colleagues while playing an engaging game.

The method is quite simple: to bring together, in easily accessible form, some of the questions that would move the hearts and minds of the players in search of truth.

Truth is not an ABSOLUTE! The game is a mirror, reflecting who you are becoming as you penetrate the many levels of the TRUTH.

Do not take life too seriously, you will never get out of it alive.
~ E. Hubbard.

We have quoted thoughts, old and new, that we found especially illuminated the material and provided humor that lends perspective to some of the more challenging questions.

This is not a game of conclusion, but one of evolution.
~ F.B.

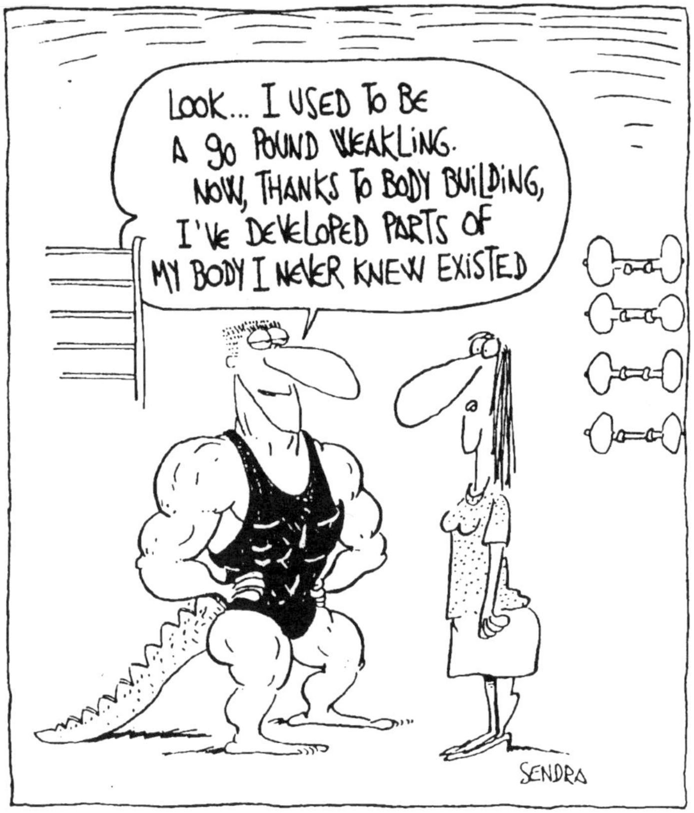
LOOK... I USED TO BE A 90 POUND WEAKLING. NOW, THANKS TO BODY BUILDING, I'VE DEVELOPED PARTS OF MY BODY I NEVER KNEW EXISTED
SENDRA

1 The Body

The Image of the Body

Though we travel the world over to find the beautiful,
we must carry it with us or we find it not.

~ *Ralph Waldo Emerson (1803-1883)*

1. Do you like your body? Describe it.

2. What is it that you like best about your body? What is your weight and height?

3. What is it that you like least about your body? Describe any particular feature, like scars, tattoos, or deformities. Are you overweight?

4. Have you ever thought about changing your physical appearance? What would you change? Describe the body that you would like to have.

5. Which one of the following statements do you think is true?

My body is attractive to other people.

My body is very attractive.

My body is sexually magnetic.

People are indifferent towards my body.

My body is repulsive to others.

My body is beautiful.

My body is ugly.

6. What is the first thing that comes to mind when you think about your body? Respond with the first thing that comes to mind:

hair

eyes

mouth

liver

nose

face

arms

hands

breasts

ass

legs

feet

continued on next page

skin

color

smell

teeth

heart

ears

clitoris

penis

testes

vagina

shoulders

belly

bones

hips

throat

7. Do you fart? Where and under what circumstances? Do you mind if somebody farts in front of you?

8. Describe your strongest bodily smells.

9. Describe the type of body you like in a partner. How is your partner similiar or different?

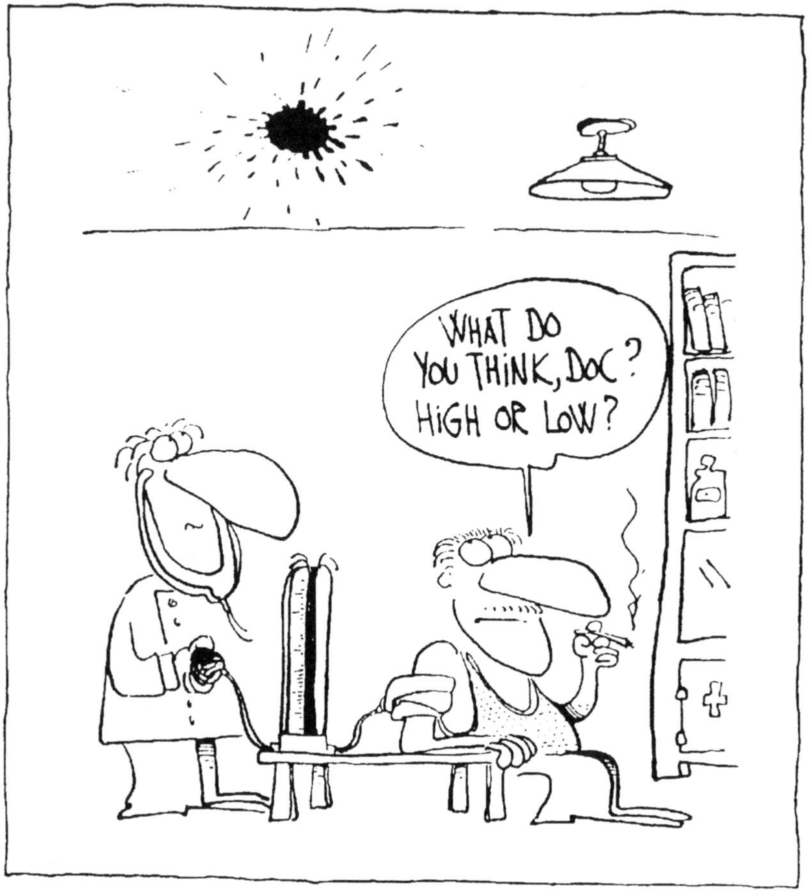
WHAT DO YOU THINK, DOC? HIGH OR LOW?

THE BODY

Functioning of the Body

The art of medicine consists of amusing the patient while nature cures the disease.

~ Voltaire (Francoise Marie Arouet) (1694-1778)

1. How is your body currently functioning? Is it:

Energetic	↔	*Lethargic*
Quick	↔	*Slow*
Agile	↔	*Clumsy*
Rigid	↔	*Flexible*
Strong	↔	*Weak*
Active	↔	*Lazy*

2. What sort of exercise, if any, do you do to keep your body in shape? What sort of exercises would you prefer to do? Do you do them? Why or why not?

3. What is the difference in the activity level of your body at work and in your spare time? How and when does your body rest? How many hours do you sleep each day?

4. Do you like to dance? When was the last time you danced? Describe the scene and your feelings at that moment.

5. Are you healthy or sick?

6. Is your body a source of suffering or of pleasure? Is your body sad or joyful?

7. In a man, which part of the body do you look at first? In a woman, which part of the body do you look at first?

8. (F) How are your menstrual periods? Are they regular? (M) Do you ever have trouble getting on erection? Explain.

9. In a week long period, how many days do you wake up tired or bored?

10. Describe the pleasure or problems that the following functions provide:

Eating
        Digesting
                Circulation
                        Breathing
       Sight   Urinating
           Listening   Sex
                Touching   Smell

11. Have you ever had a problem with these internal organs?

     arteries
         liver
            stomach
               heart
                 brain

Describe the problem.

12. How and where do you have your meals? Are they fast food? Sit down dining? Alone? With company? What do you like to eat and drink best? What do you dislike most?

13. Do you take drugs, legal or illegal? What kind and how often?

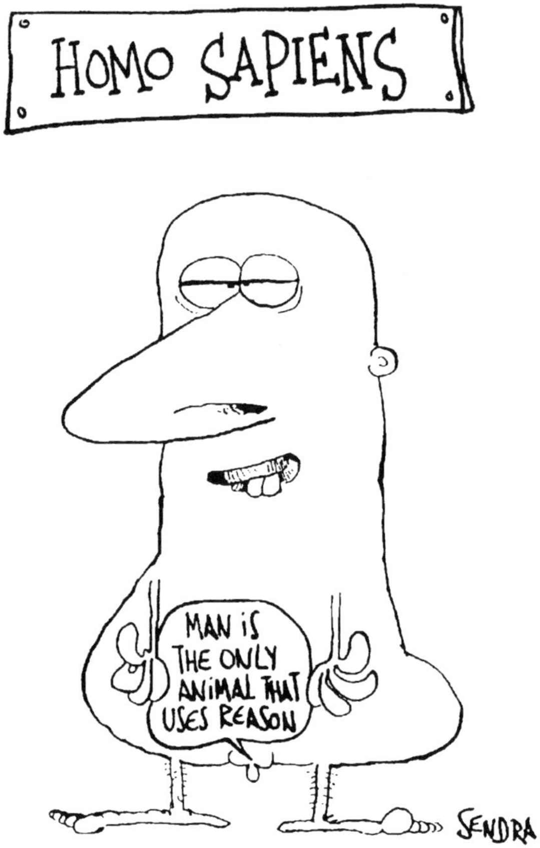
HOMO SAPIENS
MAN IS THE ONLY ANIMAL THAT USES REASON
SENDRA

THE BODY

Attitudes

You grow up the day you have the first real laugh – at yourself.
~ Ethel Barrymore

Nothing in life is to be feared. It is only to be understood.
~ Marie Curie

1. How old is your body?

2. What is death? What does it mean to you? What are your feelings about it?

3. What do you consider an old body, a young body, a mature body, an immature body?

4. What would be the ideal age at which to die?

5. How many more years do you think your body will live? How many more would you like to live?

6. When was the last time you were involved in a physical fight? Describe the circumstances and outcome.

7. Is your body: an object, a prison, a vehicle, an instrument, your destiny, or your being?

8. Have you ever examined your feet for a long period of time, looked at them carefully, studied them? Remove your shoes and observe your feet for three minutes. As you do, express honestly how you feel about your physical being, yourself, and your love relationships.

9. Do you look at your feces before you flush the toilet? What does it look like? How do you feel about it?

10. If you are a woman, how do you feel about yourself during your menstrual period? If you are a man, have you ever looked at your semen while you ejaculated? Describe it.

11. What do you think are the boundaries of your body? Do you think your body ends at your skin? Is there an astral body that goes beyond your physical body? If so, is your belief based on experience or faith?

12. Do you think you are separate from your body? On a scale from one to one hundred, with 100 being totally seperate, how separate do you think you are?

13. Do you often think about your body as if it were something that you have or as something that you are?

14. If you were about to die, would you agree to a transplant of your heart, lungs, liver or pancreas?

SUCH IS LIFE, MATILDA... OLD PEOPLE FEEL THAT YEARS FLY BY, AND KIDS BELIEVE MONTHS NEVER END.

HOW OLD ARE YOU?

I'M THAT AGE IN WHICH YEARS FLY BY AND MONTHS NEVER END

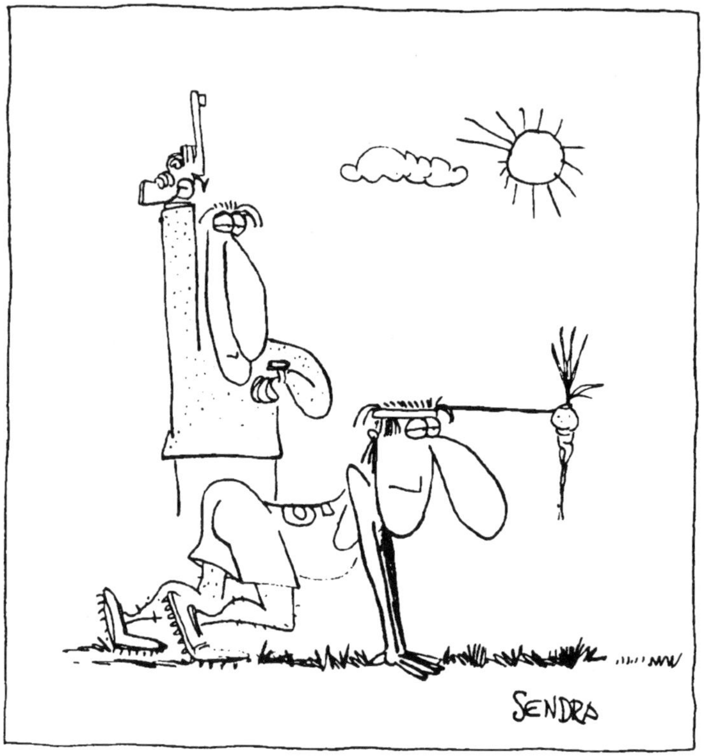
SENDRA

PERSONALITY

(General)

In each human heart are a tiger, a pig, an ass and a nightingale.
Diversity of character is due to their unequal activity.
~ *Ambrose Pierce*

There's one way to find out if a man is honest – ask him.
If he says "yes", you know he is a crook.
~ *Groucho Marx*

1. Describe your personality.

2. Name three of your personality traits that you like most.

3. Name three traits of your personality that you dislike most.

4. What is it that makes you happy and unhappy? Name two or three examples of each.

5. What are your basic 5 principles? Rate from 1-100 how you live according to them with 100 being "completely".

6. Name the opposite of the 5 principles you described above. In your daily living, which do you follow the most: your principles or their opposites? Why?

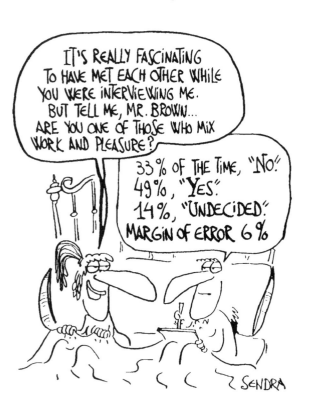

7. In your opinion, what is the best talent that you possess? What talent do you wish most to possess?

8. What is your purpose in life?

9. Would you ever go to an X-rated movie theater, walk up to the ticket booth alone, buy a ticket and go in to watch the movie?

10. Of the people in the room, which one do you consider the most extravagant?

11. Which person in the room do you think was probably a kleptomaniac when he or she was a child?

12. Which person in the room do you think is probably a hypochondriac?

13. Which person in the room has the most distorted view of your personality? Why?

14. Of the people in the room, which one loses in the most gracious manner?

15. Who is the most assertive person in the room?

16. Which of the following factors do you use to make your decisions?

your heart
      your head
            your pocketbook

Explain.

17. When you are feeling really BAD, would you say you are?

paranoid
      depressed
            hostile
                or?
Explain.

18. Which of the people in the room do you think gossips the most? Why?

19. If it could be done in total anonymity, which person in the room do you think would be most likely to sell themselves for money? Explain.

20. Rate yourself 1-100 on the following qualities with 1 being very low/few and 100 being very high/many:

as a listener
      having feelings of guilt
           possessing a sense of humor
        as a poker player
     moodiness
irritability
     needing to be the center of attention
            maturity
              self-confidence
          aggressiveness
        ambition
     stubbornness
courageousness
      social polish
        spontaneity
         efficiency
           materialism
             envy

21. Would you argue with a policeman about an unfair ticket?

22. If you were going to go into therapy, which type would you choose?

Faith Healing   *Jungian*
Freudian   *New Age Short Therapies*   *Gestalt*
Primal Scream?   *a nice chat*

23. Rate the following in order of preference:

having an exquisite gourmet dinner

having sex

buying clothes at one of the world's finest department stores.

24. When you are worried, what percentage of your worries do you share with others? With whom?

25. If you could choose to live anywhere in the world, where would it be?

26. If someone wrote a book about you, what would be an appropriate title?

27. If you could have anything in the world for your birthday, what would it be?

28. Name your favorite:

movie

song

politician

sport

hobby

29. Name three things in the world that you are the most thankful for.

30. What is your worst habit?

31. If you were invisible and could go anywhere in the world, where would you go?

32. Name six famous people that you would like to meet.

33. What would you do if you found $5,000 in bills on the street? Would you spend it? On what?

34. How do describe yourself to someone who doesn't know you?

35. If you could take any three people with you on a trip around the world, whom would you choose to take? Only one?

36. If you were moving to another country and limited to three of your personal possessions, what would you take with you?

37. If you discovered that you were going to reincarnate as an animal and could choose, which animal would you become? Which animal would you least like to become?

DOC... I'VE BEEN TOLD THAT YOU'VE DONE RESEARCH ON ORGANIC MATERIALS RESISTANCE. WHAT CONCLUSION HAVE YOU COME TO?

THAT FLESH IS WEAK, DOCTOR

SENDRA

38. If you were going to open a store, what kind of store would it be?

39. Do you have a special room in your house? If so, describe it. If not, why not?

40. Who do you consider to be lucky?

41. What do you value more: the moment of happiness or your memories of it?

42. Do you prefer individual or team sports?

43. Would you accept $10,000,000 in cash to leave your country, family and friends for 20 years?

44. If you could choose to have either your body or only your brain age, which would you age?

45. Describe what you would consider to be a perfect day.

46. If at your death, you knew that you could greatly benefit humanity by leaving your estate to a foundation, would you do it knowing that your family would then have to look after themselves?

47. Would you prefer to give 20 million dollars anonymously to benefit many or to get $500,000 for yourself?

48. Which of your belongings do you treasure the most? Explain.

49. How much money would it take for you to play a round of Russian roulette?

50. If you could choose the way that you were going to die, but doing so meant that you would live one year less, would you opt to choose? What would be your preferred way to die?

51. When you tell a story of your past, do you exaggerate or minimize the events?

52. On a scale of 0% - 100%, how much of your life do you think you have control over?

53. If you could have one servant, which of the following would it be?

a cook

a chauffeur

a housekeeper

a masseuse

personal secretary

If you had to be a servant, which of the above would you choose to be?

54. Would you enjoy spending one complete month in absolute comfort in a beautiful setting, even if you had to spend it in solitude?

55. If you could slow down your aging process and live to be 2000 years old, would you do it?

56. If you discovered an absolutely beautiful beach and then discovered that it was a nudist beach, would you leave or stay? If you'd stay, would you undress, walk around, and swim?

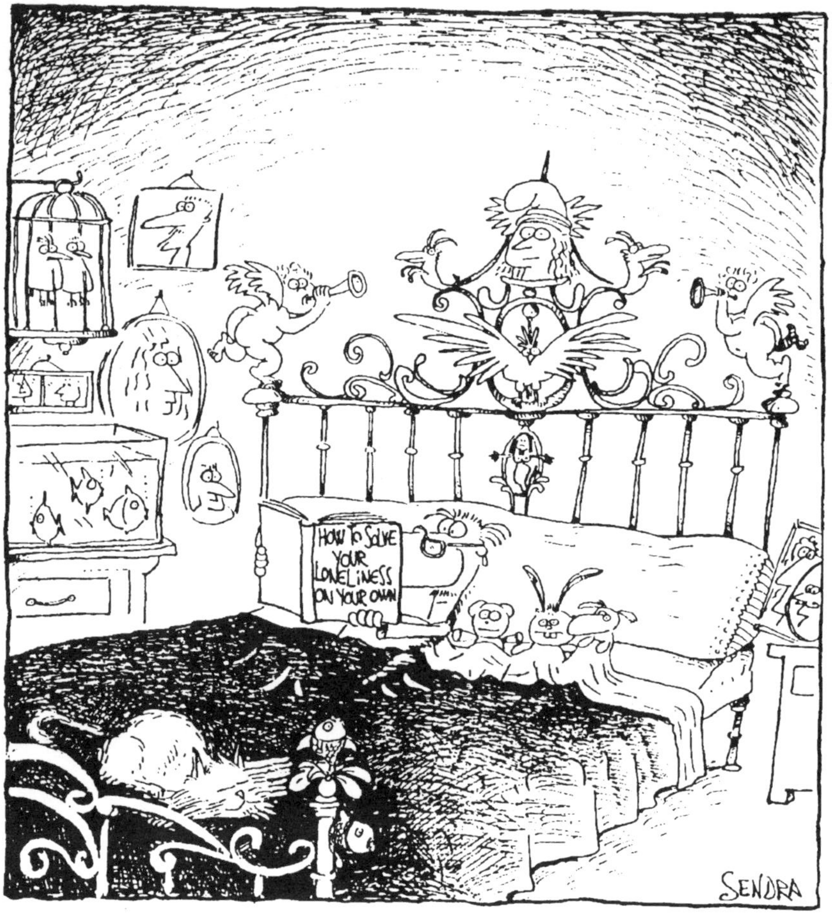
HOW To SOLVE YOUR LONELINESS ON YOUR OWN
SENDRA

Aspects of Personality

The Affective Domain

The heart has its reasons which reason does not understand.

~ Blaise Pascal (1623 - 1662)

1. What is required for you to be happy? On a scale from 1–100, with 100 being ecstatic, how would you rate your own happiness? Describe the most joyful scene you have ever lived.

2. Of the few people in your life with whom you have become most intimate, have any of them gotten to know your true nature? Explain.

3. Name five people that know your truest feelings about things.

4. Do you think it is possible to successfully lie to someone about your feelings? Have you ever done it? Explain.

5. Do you consider emotions a weakness of inferior beings or a characteristic of more highly evolved individuals?

6. Have you ever killed a living creature?

A fly?

      A mouse?

           A cat?

              A bird?

                  A human being?

If so, describe how you killed it and how you felt.

7. How and when did you fall in love last? Describe it.

8. Have you ever done something that you felt was courageous? When? Describe what you did.

9. Of the people in the room, which one has a character most similar to your own? Describe the similarities.

10. If someone wrote a book about you, what would they title it? Would it be a comedy or a drama?

11. When was the last time you got goosebumps?

12. When was the last time you really yelled at somebody? Describe.

13. When was the last time you got in a fistfight? Describe.

14. Do you like to talk about your past or prefer to keep it a secret?

15. What thing or event has changed your life in the most dramatic way? Describe the situation. Explain your feelings.

16. If you knew that you were going to die in one year, what would you change about your life?

17. Since you were fourteen years old, what is the three-year period in which you have grown the most?

18. What would you change about the way you were raised? If you have children, have you tried to make those changes in the way you've raised them? How successful have you been in those improvements?

19. Describe the conditions surrounding the last time you were depressed.

20. Describe the last time you felt frustrated.

21. When you are worried, what percentage of your worries do you share with others?

        5%
            15%
                30
                    or?

What is the biggest worry you have in your life right now?

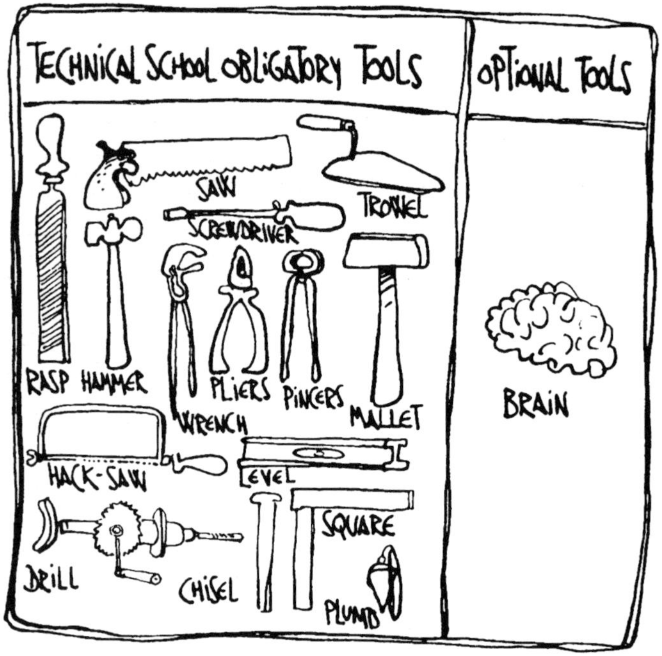
TECHNICAL SCHOOL OBLIGATORY TOOLS
OPTIONAL TOOLS
SAW
TROWEL
SCREWDRIVER
RASP
HAMMER
PLIERS
PINCERS
WRENCH
MALLET
BRAIN
HACK-SAW
LEVEL
SQUARE
DRILL
CHISEL
PLUMB

Aspects of Personality

Intelligence

We can escape from the level of society,
but not from the level of intelligence to which we were born.
~ Randall Jarrell

1. What is it to be intelligent?

2. Are you intelligent? On a scale from 1-10, where would you place yourself if 1 is imbecile and 10 is a genius? Why? Explain.

3. Do you think there is anything you can do to improve your intelligence?

4. Have you ever done anything to improve your intelligence? What did you do? When?

5. Have you made plans to enhance your intelligence? How do you plan to do it? When?

6. Rank the people in the room from the most intelligent to the least.

7. Do you trust your first impressions?

8. When was the last time your first impression was wrong?

9. What has occurred recently to complicate your life?

10. If you could choose to have either your body or only your brain age, which would you choose?

11. How much is: $4 \times 7 - 7 + 36 \times 3 + 687 =$ _____?

12. In which field do you think of yourself as very intelligent? In which field do you think of yourself as having average intelligence? In which fields do you consider yourself dumb?

13. If by sacrificing 35% of your current intellectual ability you could extend your life by 30 years, would you do it? How much of your intelligence would you give up in order to live longer?

14. Which of the following would you prefer: a government run by a superior intelligence, 250 IQ, with the ability to kill its opposition, or a government run by an intelligence of about 100 IQ that couldn't harm a fly?

7 Aspects of Personality

Spirituality

Seek not to understand that you may believe, but believe that you may understand.
~ Saint Augustine

1. Do you believe in the existence of a spirit that continues to live after you die? If so, on what do you base this belief?

2. What is religion to you? How would you describe it? On a scale of 1-100, with 100 being extremely religious, how religious do you think you are?

3. Describe three religious figures that you admire. Why do you admire them?

4. In your opinion, are some religions true and others false? How do you know?

5. On a scale of 1-100, with 100 being "I can teach it", how would you rank your knowledge of other religions? Which 3 do you know most about?

6. Which one of the following describes you best?

follow the religion of my parents

rebel against the religion of my father or family

converted to another religion

don't believe in or belong to any religion

7. Would you kill another human being because of your faith?

8. Define the fundamental principles upon which your system of belief is based.

9. What are the three worst sins of your society?

10. What do you consider to be your three worst sins?

11. Do you believe there are higher laws operating in the universe? What are these laws?

12. Are you a sensitive person? Why or why not? Explain.

13. What are the qualities you look for in a friend?

14. Do you trust your first impressions about people? When was the last time your first impression turned out to be wrong?

15. What does "security" mean to you? Do you fight for it? If so, how?

16. What kind of feelings do you have when you are with someone who doesn't speak your language?

17. What invention do you think the world needs most these days?

18. When was the last time you were involved in an activity that involved your mind, body, and soul?

19. Describe the moments of greatest solitude in your life.

20. What are the three most important things in your life?

21. If you were going to die in a week, how would you spend it? If it were going to happen within 3 hours, who would you like to speak to and why?

22. How do you feel about aging? Can you imagine yourself at 97? If so, describe your feelings.

23. What is the main difference between Buddhism, Judaism, Christianity and Islam? What are their siimilarities?

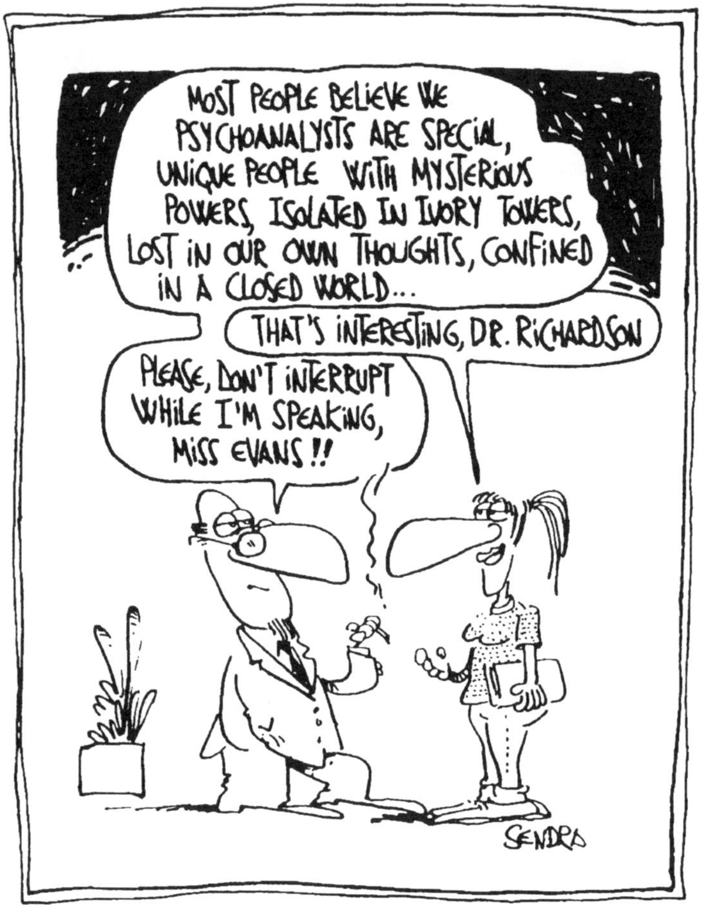
MOST PEOPLE BELIEVE WE PSYCHOANALYSTS ARE SPECIAL, UNIQUE PEOPLE WITH MYSTERIOUS POWERS, ISOLATED IN IVORY TOWERS, LOST IN OUR OWN THOUGHTS, CONFINED IN A CLOSED WORLD...
THAT'S INTERESTING, DR. RICHARDSON
PLEASE, DON'T INTERRUPT WHILE I'M SPEAKING, MISS EVANS!!
SENDRA

Mirrors of Personality

The Individual

I know well what I am fleeing from but not what I am in search of.

~ Michel de Montaigne (1533 - 1592)

1. Do you consider yourself a complete human being? On a scale of 1-100, with 100 being complete, rank your wholeness.

2. Do you think it would be possible for another person to be virtually identical to you? Could a person be 99% identical? 85%? 70%?

3. What is the fundamental difference that distinguishes your 3 best friends? Name the friends and explain the differences.

4. Imagine a world populated by millions and millions of individuals that were cloned from you, identical with you. Describe the major characteristics of that world: economics, personal relations, government, education, etc.

5. Would you name your child for yourself? Have you ever felt pride or shame in your first or last name? Have you ever thought of changing it? Have you?

6. What would you do if one day you saw your mother being unfaithful to your father and on the next day your father came to you and told you what a wonderful, honest person your mother was?

7. Have you ever thought about suicide? Have you ever attempted it? What were the circumstances?

8. If you were in a sinking ship and you could save either your mother or your father, but not both of them, which would you save?

9. How would you describe yourself to someone who doesn't know you?

10. Of the people in the room, which one do you think is the most emotionally stable?

11. Of the people in the room, which one do you know the least about? Ask him/her a question.

12. When was the last time you yelled at someone? Why did you do it?

13. Are you able to accept help when you need it?

14. Do you make sure that you always thank the people who help you?

15. Do you get upset when someone you have helped doesn't acknowledge your assistance?

16. In what ways do you consider yourself childish? Explain.

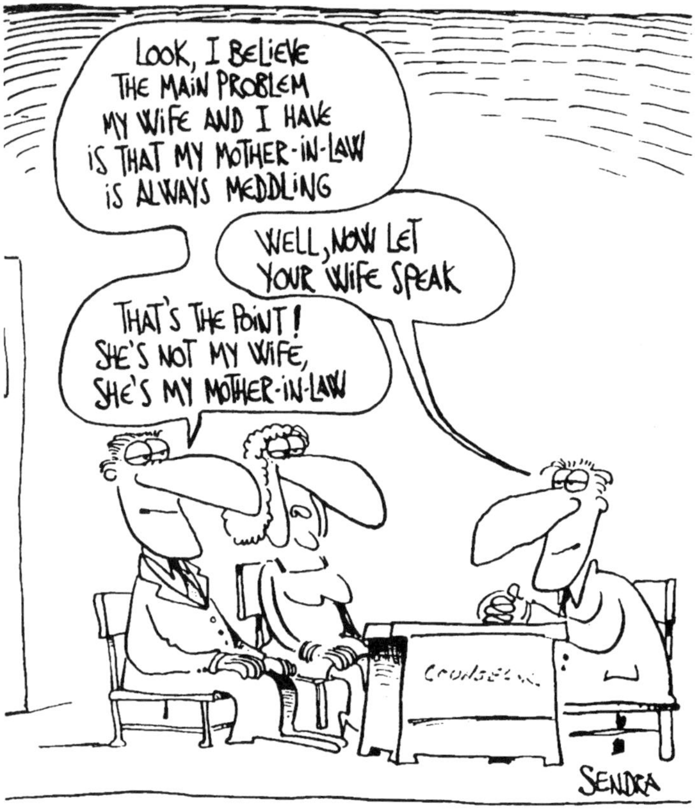
LOOK, I BELIEVE THE MAIN PROBLEM MY WIFE AND I HAVE IS THAT MY MOTHER-IN-LAW IS ALWAYS MEDDLING
WELL, NOW LET YOUR WIFE SPEAK
THAT'S THE POINT! SHE'S NOT MY WIFE, SHE'S MY MOTHER-IN-LAW
SENDRA

Mirrors of Personality

The Family

If you cannot get rid of the family skeleton, you may as well make it dance.
~ George Bernard Shaw

1. Which member of your family knows you the best? Which member of your family has the most distorted view of you?

2. Have you ever judged your parents? How do you feel when you judge them? Name three positive and three negative personality traits that each possesses. Of the characteristics that you listed for your parents, which ones do you possess?

3. In your life, have you chosen to be like your parents or different from them? Explain.

4. If you could have chosen the family into which you were born, what would it be like? Describe it.

5. Name two famous people that you would have liked to have as parents. Would you like to have a life like theirs?

6. Which of the following family types would you prefer to be born into? Which would you prefer your children to be born into?

- a family of elephants where the females care for the children and the males group together on their own.

- a family of cattle where the bull is the chief and guardian of the territory and also of the females.

- a family of penguins where the male sacrifices himself to care for the eggs while the female relaxes.

- a pack of wolves where the female is totally on her own while the male hunts.

- a family of eagles where the male and female share a nest and the caretaking of their offspring.

- a family of fish where there is no recognized parenthood.

- a family of monkeys where the strongest one mates with the female of his choice and there is no recognized paternity.

Mirrors of Personality

7. Describe briefly the relationship between your mother and father.

8. What opinion did your mother's family have of your father?

9. What opinion did your father's family have of your mother?

10. In one sentence, state what the following people think about you:

mother

      father

            brothers and/or sisters

                  spouse

                    children

11. If someone in your immediate family were suffering from mental illness, would you have them live with you and share your life? Or would you put them in an institution? Would the answer be different if you knew there was no cure?

12. When you were a child, what was the most frequent theme of conversation in your family? What was the subject spoken of least? Now that you are an adult, have the conversations changed? How have they changed?

13. Can you easily say what you feel about your family while you are in their presence?

14. What is it that you wanted most when you were a child? Did you acquire or achieve it?

15. Do you think you have had a more satisfying sexual life that your father and mother?

16. Name the three best things you have received from your family.

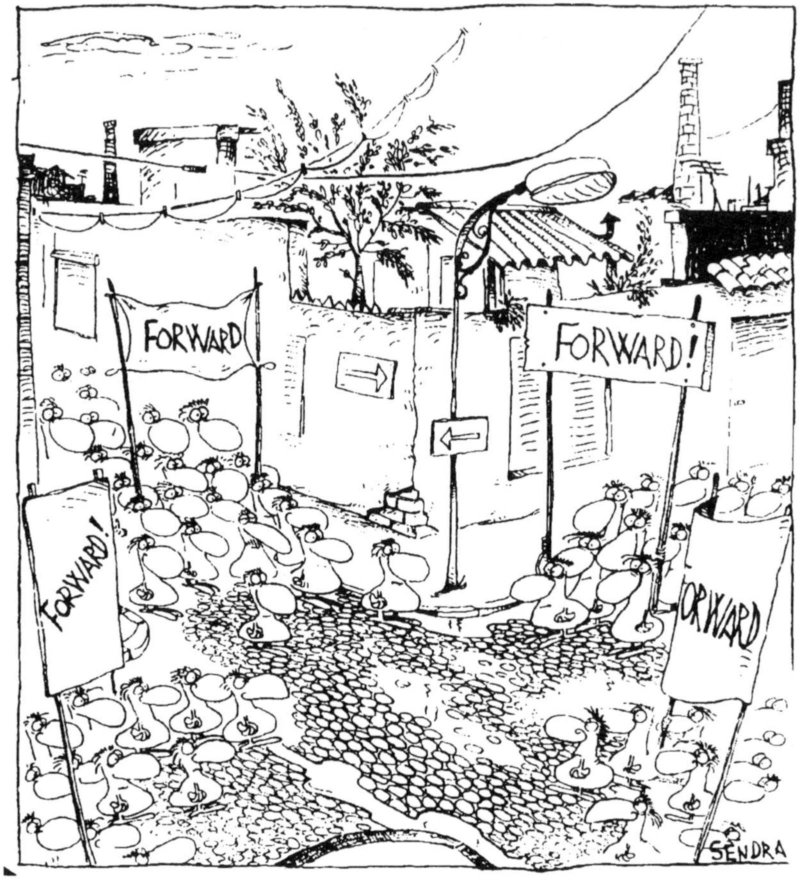
FORWARD
FORWARD!
FORWARD!
FORWARD
SENDRA

10 Mirrors of Personality

Society

Society attacks early when the individual is helpless.
~ B.F. Skinner

1. Mention three political figures you admire and tell why you admire them.

2. Which two people in the room do you think would like to get to know each other better? Explain.

3. Which person in the room has the most negative view of you as a person? Which one has the most positive view?

4. Which person in the room is the most gracious when they lose at something? Describe by mimicking that person.

5. Of the people in the room, which one do you think has the most interesting fantasy life? Imagine one, and describe it.

6. Of the people in the room, which one do you think accepts a mistake the easiest?

7. Of the people in the room, which one do you think will have fantasies of wild revenge for the things said about him or her today? Are you afraid of this possibility? If so, does this fear affect your answers?

8. Which person in the room is the most pleasure seeking? Explain why you think this.

9. Which person in the room is the most assertive? Act out an example.

10. Which person in the room do you know the least about? What would you like to know about him or her?

11. Which person in the room do you think likes to gossip the most? Explain.

12. Which person in the room would be the most likely to sell his or her favors for money if it could be done in total anonymity? Why do you think so?

13. What is your relationship with your neighbors?

14. When you are not with your friends, what do you think they say about you?

15. If you were to die tonight, is there anything you would regret not having said? What? To whom?

16. In your life, how often are you the center of attention? On a scale from 1-100 with 1 being no attention and 100 being constant attention, rate yourself.

17. Of the people in the room, which one shares the least of his or her private life?

18. Define with one brief phrase each of the following groups:

Russians   Chinese   Spaniards   Brits

    Italians   Dutch   Poles

Scots   Germans   S.Africans   Turks

        Frenchmen

        Mexicans

Californians

        Bostonians

Canadians

        Brazilians

Argentinians

        Cubans

Texans

        New

Yorkers

Hindus

        Ethiopians

Caaribbean Islanders

        Israelis

Japanese

        Aussies

19. What do you think of the following groups of people?

Communists

Nazis

Jews

Arabs

Hispanics

Latinos

Whites

Blacks

Chinese

Catholics

Muslims

Protestants

Buddhists

Liberals

Conservatives

Homosexuals

20. Describe your immediate society and explain your role in it.

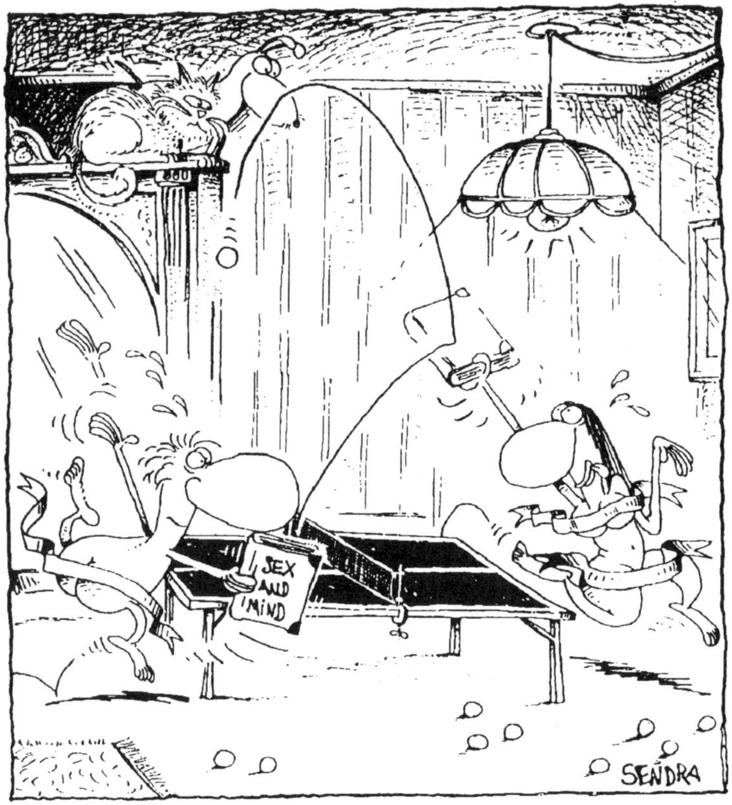
SEX
AND
MIND
SENDRA

11 Sex, Power & Money

Sex

Sexual pleasure, wisely used and not abused, may prove the stimulus and liberator of our finest and most exalted activities.

~ Havelock Ellis

1. Are you satisfied with your sexual life? Explain.

2. On a sexual satisfaction scale of 1-10, where would you place your sexual life if 1 equals no satisfaction and 10 is ecstasy?

3. Do you have a regular sexual mate? Describe him/her.

4. Explain why you do or do not have a regular sexual mate.

5. Have you ever thought about changing mates? Describe the situation. Did you do it?

6. Which of the following is preferable?

celibacy

to masturbate alone

to be part of a couple in total fidelity

to occasionally be part of a couple

to participate in group sex

7. Which of the previous conditions gives you more pleasure?

8. What do you think about homosexuals and lesbians? What do you think about heterosexuals?

9. (If heterosexual) Have you ever had any homosexual or lesbian impulses? If so, when was the last time? (If homosexual) Have you ever had any heterosexual impulses? If so, when was the last time?

10. Do you have homosexual friends? How do you feel about them? Do you have heterosexual friends? How do you feel about them?

11. Do you feel any kind of shame or self-consciousness while you are answering sex-related questions? Why?

12. Are you ashamed when you recognize how sensitive you are to sex related questions?

13. Describe the sexual behavior that satisfies you the most.

14. Describe the sexual behaviors that you practice the most.

15. Are you able to verbalize your sexual desires? Describe one.

16. Does your sexual partner verbalize his or her sexual desires? If yes, do you enjoy it? If no, do you wish s/he would?

17. At what age do you think you will stop having sex?

18. What is your primary motive for having sex?

reproduction

pleasure

instinct

communication

mystical union

19. Have you ever used external or imaginary stimulation during sex? (videos, imagining a different partner, etc.)?

20. Have you ever experienced any of the following during a sexual encounter:

> *impotence*
>
> *frigidity*
>
> *premature ejaculation*
>
> *retarded ejaculation*
>
> *nymphomania?*

Why do you think you experienced the above?

21. Have you ever had sex in exchange for the following?

> *money*
>
> *trips or holidays*
>
> *fame*
>
> *more power*
>
> *social status or prestige*
>
> *acceptance by another person*
>
> *acceptance by a group*

22. (M) Do you consider yourself a macho kind of man? Explain.
(F) Do you consider yourself a feminist? Explain.

23. Name some of the things you consider to be sexual perversions. Of these, how many have you practiced? Have you ever fantasized about any of these perversions? Which ones?

24. Do you consider yourself sexy?

25. On a scale of 1-10, where would you place yourself if 1 is totally unattractive and 10 is a knockout?

26. What are the erotic points on your body? Name at least five.

27. Is it better to be a man or a woman? Why? Would you have preferred to be a different sex?

28. Do you think it is better not to talk about sex? Why or why not?

29. What are the characteristics of the men and women that you usually attract? Which are you usually attracted to?

30. What do you think of prostitution? Have you ever had sex with a prostitute?

31. If you found out that your sexual partner were frustrated, would you mind if he or she experimented with others?

32. Would you mind if your mate or sexual partner had sex with someone else if it were part of a therapeutic sexual program?

33. If you had to choose between losing all your money or becoming impotent, which would you choose?

34. On a scale of 1-100, would you rate your sexual experience as a positive thing in your life? On the same scale, rate it as a negative thing.

35. What are the three best pieces of advice you would give to a child about sex?

36. On a scale of 1-100 with 1 being totally dishonest and 100 being completely honest, rate the honesty of the answers you have given about sex.

Evolution of the War on Cockroaches
CRO-MAGNON
-PITECANTROPUS-
HOMO-FABER
SUMERIOS
-EGIPCIOS-
-GRECIA-
-ROMA-
-CHINA-
-ISLAM-
-CRUZADO-
-NOBLEZA FEUDAL-
SUUU
-INCAS-
-IMPERIOS EUROPEOS-
NCL POW.

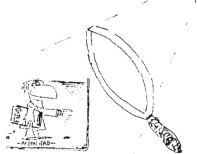

12 Sex, Power, & Money

Power

Power tends to corrupt and absolute power corrupts absolutely.
~ Lord Acton

1. What is "power" to you?

2. On a scale of 1 to 10, how would you rank your actual degree of power in the world if 1 is powerless and 10 is extremely powerful? What would a 10 be like for you?

3. Define impotence. Describe a situation where you felt impotent.

4. Would you like to have more power than you have now? What is preventing you from having more power?

5. Have you done anything lately to acquire more power? Have you thought about it? Explain.

6. What is the worst thing you have done in order to get more power?

7. According to you, which of the following people are most powerful?

Bill Clinton

your mother

The Pope

Bill Gates

Queen Elizabeth

your father

Bob Dylan

The Dalai Lama

Madonna

Gabriel Garcia Marquez

Sadam Hussein

Hillary Rodham Clinton

Fidel Castro

Nelson Mandela

Oprah Winfrey

Boris Yeltsin

8. Do you liked to be served by other people? Do you have servants?

9. Do you serve anyone? Do you like to serve other people?

10. How do you relate to your subordinates? Do you think you are equal or superior? Do you act like an equal in order to make them feel good?

11. Do you think your subordinates will ever reach the kind of position you have?

12. Do you treat your subordinates in an authoritarian or condescending way?

13. Do you think a pure race is superior to a mixed race?

14. Do you think some races are superior to others? If so, in what ways?

15. Would you ever marry or have as a companion someone from another race or religion?

16. In your life, would you choose to be the head of a mouse or the tail of a lion?

17. Do you vote in elections? If so, what party do you vote for?

18. Do you believe in democracy? Why or why not? Do you think it is fair when an election results in 49% vs. 51% and the 51% governs everyone? Explain.

19. Do you think that power corrupts? Have you ever been corrupted?

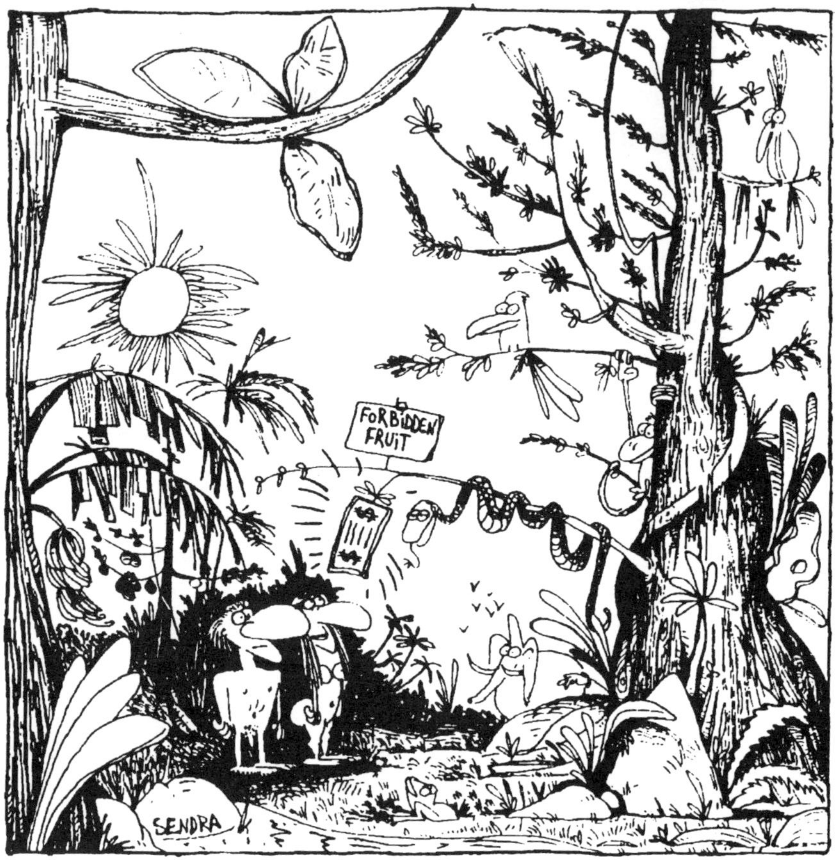
FORBIDDEN FRUIT
SENDRA

Sex, Power, & Money

Money

Money is a terrible master but an excellent servant.

~ P.T. Barnum (1810-1891)

1. How much money do you have?

2. How much money would you like to have?

3. Do you feel like you need more money, or do you think you have enough?

4. What is the most unpleasant thing you have ever done for money?

5. How much do you feel your life is worth? Do you have a life insurance policy? If so, for how much?

6. Would you play a serious game of Russian roulette for $10,000,000?

7. On a scale of 1-10, with 1 being the lowest, at which level of the socio-economic scale are you?

8. On a scale of 1-10, rank each of the players according to a socio-economic scale with 1 being the lowest.

9. Have you ever suffered for money? Explain why and when and describe the situation.

10. When was the last time you had a family conflict about finances? Describe.

11. Have you ever loved another person for their money? Have you ever hated another person because of money? Explain.

12. Have you ever felt the desire to take revenge because of money?

13. Do you think money corrupts? Have you ever been corrupted by money?

14. Do you think the ideal "Happy Man or Woman" is someone with a lot of money or no money? Explain.

15. To what degree does money bring happiness to you? Rate the degree from 1-100, with 1 being none. How much money do you need for happiness?

16. What percentage of your happiness is caused by the following:

> *health*
>
> *money*
>
> *love*

17. Do you envy other people's wealth?

18. Do you show your wealth or do you hide it?

19. Are you proud of the money that you have?

20. With whom do you compare yourself, the rich or the poor?

21. Have you lied for money? Describe the situation. Are you sure about your answer to the previous question? (taxes, loans, self-image, etc.)

22. Does money give you security? Do you feel depressed, unworthy or empty if you don't have money?

23. Does your self-worth depend on the amount of money you have? Fantasize losing everything you own. How would you feel about yourself and society?

24. Do you like to be envied or admired because of your wealth?

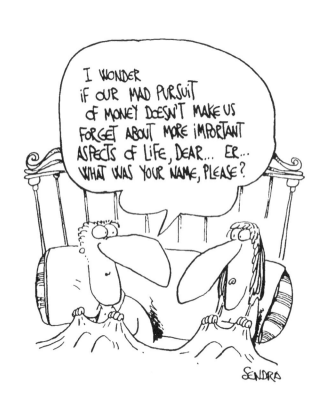

25. What would you do if you won a million dollars in the lottery?

26. Would the world be better without money?

27. What amount of money would you steal if you were sure of not being caught?

28. Would you steal money if only your family knew you were doing it?

29. Is stealing from a bureaucracy different than stealing from individuals? Explain.

30. How have you made your money?

31. Do you feel pleasure when you receive a large amount of money, such as three times your monthly income? Explain.

32. Does it make you feel bad or uncomfortable to pay out a large sum of money? What is a large sum of money?

33. Do you think it would be desirable to save up enough money so that you could live off the interest?

34. Do you think you receive a fair amount of money for the work you do? How much would be fair?

35. What do you think of people who are poor? What do you think of millionaires? Describe your interactions with each.

36. How do you behave or express yourself when you are with people who have a lot of money? How do you behave or express yourself when you are with people who have nothing? Is there a difference? What is the difference?

37. How do you see your old age in terms of money?

38. Do you save? Do you have insurance?

39. What do you think of the character Robin Hood? Explain. Is it fair to steal from the unfair?

40. Do you think it is fair to pay taxes? If you can avoid paying taxes, do you do it?

41. Would you kill or order a killing if by doing it you would obtain enormous wealth and be certain that you would never be caught?

42. Are you afraid of poverty?

43. Which would you prefer: being independent and poor, or wealthy, but subservient to a wealthier person?

44. Do you gamble for money? Describe the last time.

45. Do you like to take risks for money?

46. What questions would you like to ask the other people in the room about their money?

14 Morals, Friendship & Work

Morals

He that is without sin among you, let him cast the first stone.

~ Jesus

1. Are you a moral person? Explain.

2. What do you understand about being moral?

3. What are the three most important things in your life?

4. Have you ever been courageous? Describe the situation.

5. Have you ever lied? If so, explain your worst lie.

6. Define freedom. From 1-100, with 1 being enslaved, how free are you? Explain.

7. What is the worst thing a parent can do to their children? Was this done to you as a child? Have you ever done it to your children or to any other child?

8. Of the people in the room with you, which ones are capable of sneaking into a movie without paying? Have you done it?

9. On a scale of 1-10, with 1 being total rejection and 10 being complete loyalty, rate your respect for traditional values.

10. Have you ever lied or cheated and felt justified? If so, describe such a situation.

11. If you knew that your child was going to be born retarded and die at the age of five, would you accept an abortion?

12. What is your worst habit?

13. Would you start a relationship that would provide total satisfaction for one year knowing your partner would die a painless death at the end of the year? Would your answer be the same if your mate betrayed and left you instead of dying?

14. If you were engaged, would you cancel the engagement if an accident were to render your betrothed a paraplegic? If you were to become disabled?

15. Do you accept the concept ofeuthanasia? Would you perform euthanasia on your father or mother?

16. If you saw someone drop $6,000 in old hundred dollar bills while getting into a new Rolls Royce and you got the license number of the car, would you make an effort to return the money?

17. If someone close to you had AIDS would you avoid that person? Would your answer change if that person were your brother?

18. What amount of money would it take for you to slaughter a cow?

19. If someone you knew well was being unfairly criticized, would you defend him/her?

20. Have you ever thought of suicide? What was the reason?

21. What punishment would you give someone who killed a beloved of yours?

22. Define the following concepts:

fear

     security

          respect

honesty

               corruption

                  tyranny

                    hypocrisy

23. Would you kill an animal in order to eat?

24. Do you think God knew Adam and Eve were going to sin? Why do you think God placed them in the garden?

25. Do you think society would improve if sexual instinct in the species were weaker?

26. What do you think about artificial insemination?

27. Would you consent to a series of genetic experiments that would result in many deformed beings if the experiments ultimately produced a super-human?

28. Would you sacrifice your life for another human being? For 10 others? For 100 human beings?

29. Do you think there are inferior races? If so, name them and explain.

30. Imagine that only one of the following individuals could survive from birth. Which one would you choose?

Einstein

Gandhi

Rockefeller

Gorbachev

31. Do you think animals have souls?

32. Do you believe that you are a son/daughter of God, a creation of God, a product of chance, or the simple result of your parents' acts? Why?

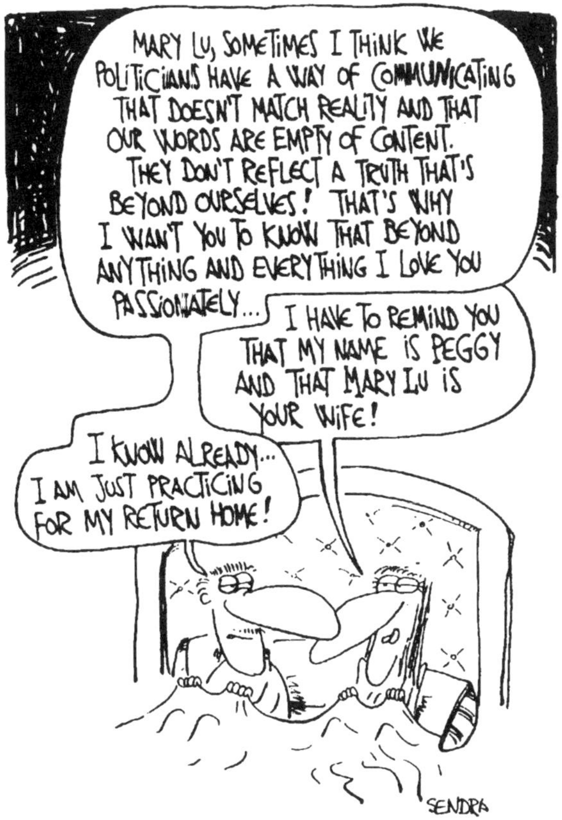
MARY LU, SOMETIMES I THINK WE POLITICIANS HAVE A WAY OF COMMUNICATING THAT DOESN'T MATCH REALITY AND THAT OUR WORDS ARE EMPTY OF CONTENT. THEY DON'T REFLECT A TRUTH THAT'S BEYOND OURSELVES! THAT'S WHY I WANT YOU TO KNOW THAT BEYOND ANYTHING AND EVERYTHING I LOVE YOU PASSIONATELY...
I HAVE TO REMIND YOU THAT MY NAME IS PEGGY AND THAT MARY LU IS YOUR WIFE!
I KNOW ALREADY... I AM JUST PRACTICING FOR MY RETURN HOME!
SENDRA

33. What do you think about abortion? Are there any conditions where you would accept it? Have you practiced it? If so, what were your circumstances and feelings?

34. If you knew that you were going to die in six months, would you be willing to be frozen now for 1,000 years in order to have a 15% possibility of being cured when awakened? Would you do it if there were a 50% chance?

35. Would you donate a kidney (while alive) to your mother, father, mate, brother, sister, child, or best friend? Do you give blood?

36. Would you receive blood that was contaminated by the AIDS virus if you were in a near fatal accident and there was no other blood available?

37. Would you subject yourself to an experiment that might leave you permanently disabled or deformed if it resulted in a lot of money for your family and progress for humanity?

38. Are you honest? On a scale from 1-10 where would you place yourself if 1 is thoroughly dishonest?

39. Are you satisfied with your rating on this scale? Why?

40. Give three words that best describe the way you are feeling right now.

41. With which person in the room would you be most willing to share your deepest, darkest secret? What is the secret?

42. Of the people in the room, which one do you think would be the most likely to sell his or her favors for money?

43. Of the people in the room, who do you think shares the least of their private lives?

44. Have you or would you cheat on a test?

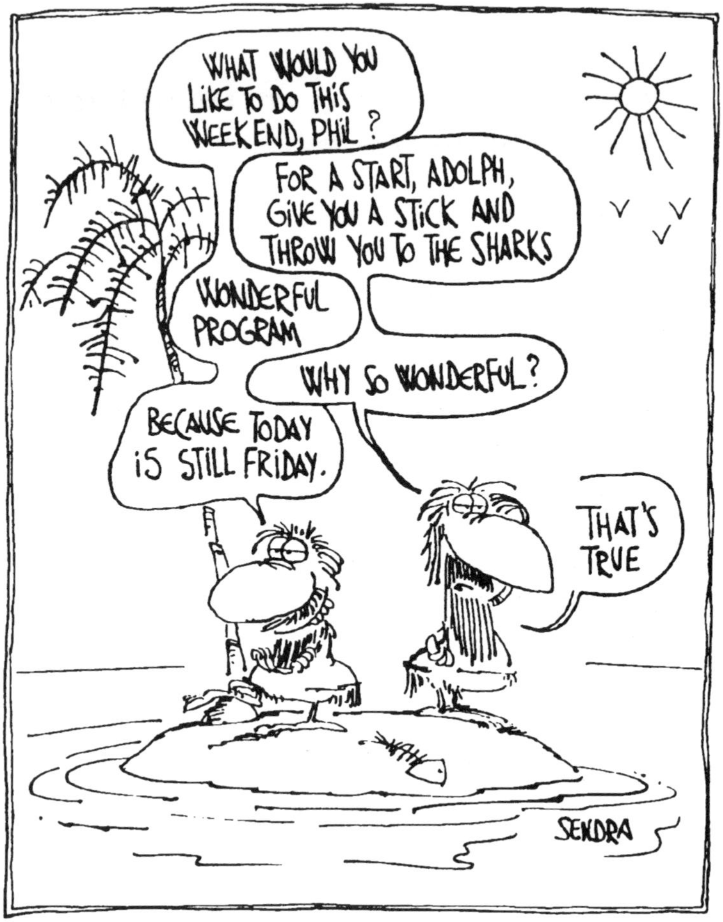
WHAT WOULD YOU LIKE TO DO THIS WEEKEND, PHIL ?
FOR A START, ADOLPH, GIVE YOU A STICK AND THROW YOU TO THE SHARKS
WONDERFUL PROGRAM
WHY SO WONDERFUL ?
BECAUSE TODAY IS STILL FRIDAY.
THAT'S TRUE
SENDRA

Morals, Friendship & Work

Friendship

True friendship comes when silence between two people is comfortable.
~ Dave Tyson Gentry

You can always tell a real friend; when you've made a fool of yourself
he doesn't feel you've done a permanent job.
~ Laurence J. Peter

1. Name (at least 3) the qualities you look for in a friend. Do you possess these qualities?

Morals, Friendship, & Work

Friendship

2. Do you consider yourself friendly? How many friends do you have? How long have these friendships lasted?

3. What is friendship to you?

4. What kind of things do you share with your friends?

money	affection
sexuality	ideas
gossip	aesthetics
worries	time
intimacy	conflicts

5. Where do you make friends?

work
neighborhood
school
family
church
hobbies
political groups

6. What would you do if you heard that a good friend was criticizing you behind your back? Would you end the friendship? Would you confront the person? Or would you do the same and talk about this friend behind his/her back?

7. Do your friends tell you honestly what they think about you? Or do they tend to tell you what you want to hear?

8. Do you consider yourself blunt, candid, afraid of misunderstandings, suspicious, cunning, generous?

9. Have you ever felt betrayed by a friendship? Describe the situation.

10. What is the most important thing a friend has ever given you? Describe the relationship with your very best friend.

11. Would you like to have more friends? If yes, what is preventing you from having them?

12. If your best friend and your mother were drowning, who would you save?

13. Of the people in the room, which one do you think makes the best friend?

14. Would you begin a relationship that would give you total satisfaction for one year if you knew at the start that your mate would die (with no pain) at the end of the year? Would you begin a relationship that would give you total satisfaction for one year if you knew at the start that your mate would betray you at the end of the year?

15. Have your intimate relationships changed since the AIDS virus became known? Explain.

16. If at your death you could greatly benefit humanity by leaving your estate to a particular foundation, would you do so knowing that your family would then have to look after themselves?

17. If you were in a relationship and on one occasion your partner cheated on you, would you want to know?

18. If you were in a relationship and on one occasion you cheated on your partner, would you tell your partner about it?

19. Who do you envy? Explain.

20. Are your friends younger or older than you?

21. If you were engaged and just before the wedding your betrothed was in an accident in which s/he became a paraplegic, would you go through with the marriage?

22. Do you believe in euthanasia?

23. Would your answer be the same if your father, mother or mate were the one to receive the mercy killing?

24. Would you like all your friends and family to tell you what they really think of you?

25. Would you want your mate to be more attractive and intelligent than you?

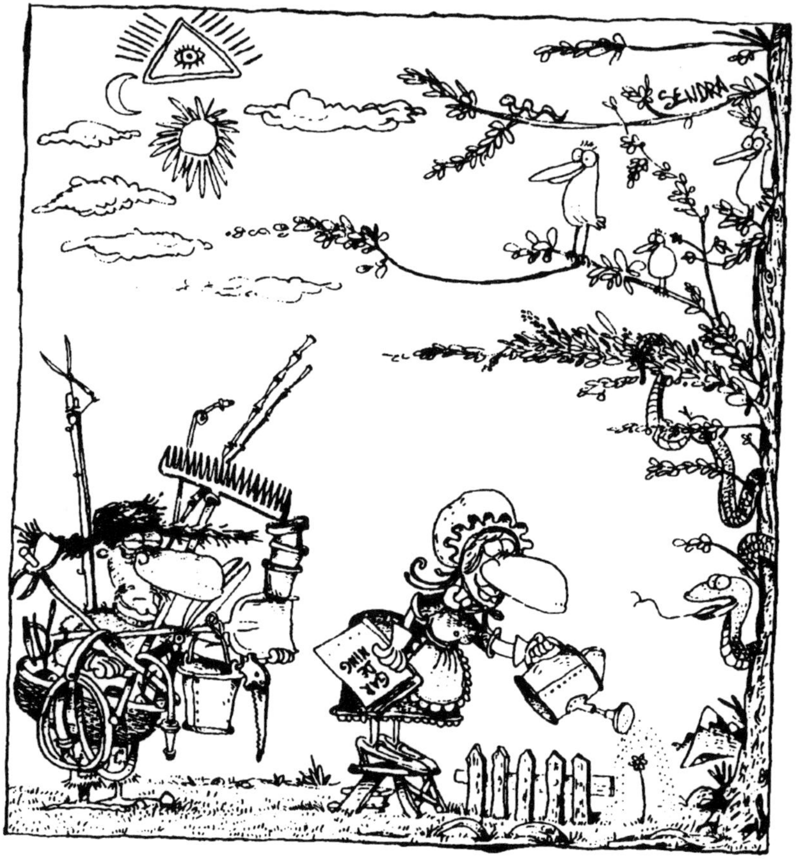
SENDRA
GAR
DE
NING

16 Morals, Friendship & Work

Work

Nothing is really work, unless you would rather be doing something else.
~ James M. Barrie

Do what you can, with what you have, where you are.
~ Theodore Roosevelt

1. What are the three things that you want to be remembered for?

2. What is your best talent? Why do you feel this way?

3. What is the thing you do best? What is the thing that gives you the most satisfaction?

4. What is your definition of success? Rate your success from 1-100.

5. If you were given a magic wand that could do anything you could imagine, what three acts would you perform first?

6. If tomorrow you could start any job that you wanted, what would it be?

7. What is your favorite sport and why?

8. Do you have spare time? What do you do with it? Do you enjoy it? Why, why not?

9. If you knew that you could become famous, what would you do?

10. If just by thinking and repeating a curse or a chant you could negatively affect other people's lives, would you use this ability?

11. If you knew for sure that the Third World War would begin in one week, what would you do before the war started?

12. If you could go into the past and change anything you wanted in history, where would you go and what would you change? Would you still go if you knew you could never come back?

13. What kind of work do you do? Do you like it? Why do you do it?

14. Have you thought of changing your work? If yes, why haven't you done it?

15. If all the financial needs of your family were taken care of, would you accept a job that offered a lot of satisfaction, but very limited income?

16. If you could be doing anything you wanted to do right at this moment, what would you choose to do? If it's not playing The Game of Truth, why aren't you doing it?

17. How much money would you ask to be paid for spending the next ten years doing one of the following?

mining in South Africa

fishing In Alaska

picking up the garbage in Tokyo

being a surgeon in the warfront

being an economist for a large bank

being a beggar in New York

being a gigolo or prostitute in Paris

being a peasant in Guatemala

being an engineer at NASA

being an actor in Hollywood

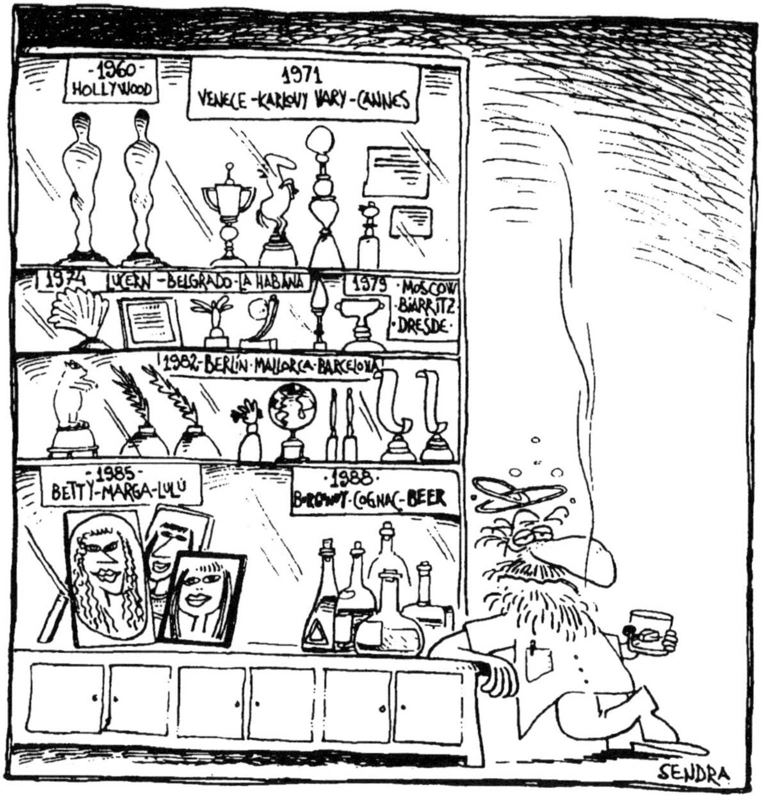
-1960-
HOLLYWOOD
1971
VENECE-KARLOVY VARY-CANNES
1974 LUCERN-BELGRADO-LA HABANA
1979 ·MOSCOW
·BIARRITZ
·DRESDE·
1982-BERLÍN·MALLORCA·BARCELONA
-1985-
BETTY-MARGA-LULÚ
·1988·
COGNAC-BEER
SENDRA

17 Image, Culture & Ecology

Image

A celebrity is a person who works hard all his life to become well known, and then wears dark glasses to avoid being recognized.
~ Fred Allen

1. What is the image that other people have of you? Name your best friend and your worst enemy. Describe the image that each has of you.

2. Would you like to be remembered after your death? How would you like to be remembered?

3. What would you like to have as an epitaph?

4. When was the last time you felt embarrassed? Describe the situation.

5. How do you feel about aging?

6. Of the people in the room, who do you think is the most similar to you? Describe three similarities.

7. Of the people in the room, which one has the most distorted view of you as a person? Answer the same question for the people you work with and in your family.

8. On a scale from 1-100, with 1 being horrible, how would you rate your physical appearance?

9. Name the person that believes your image of yourself is close to the truth? Which person believes your image is far from the truth?

10. On a scale of 1-100, how would you rate your social polish? What do you consider to be "social polish"? For which three things are you the most thankful in your life?

11. Name three famous people that you are attracted to. What is the main characteristic that each one displays? Would you like to have these characteristics? Why don't you have them?

12. If you had to be reincarnated as an animal, which one and where in the world would you choose?

13. If you were going to open a store and operate it yourself, what kind of store would it be? Describe it.

14. In your social environment, do you consider yourself: extraordinary, ordinary, special, different, unique, original, exclusive, chic, dirty, provocative, notorious, unknown, just one of the crowd?

15. Are you attracted by fame? Do you like people to notice you? Why?

16. Would you like to be famous? Describe the last time you were the center of attention.

17. What aspect of your character do you think warrants fame and recognition? Why aren't you famous now?

18. What would you be willing to do for fame? Comment on the worst thing you have done in order to be noticed.

19. What is something you would never do for fame?

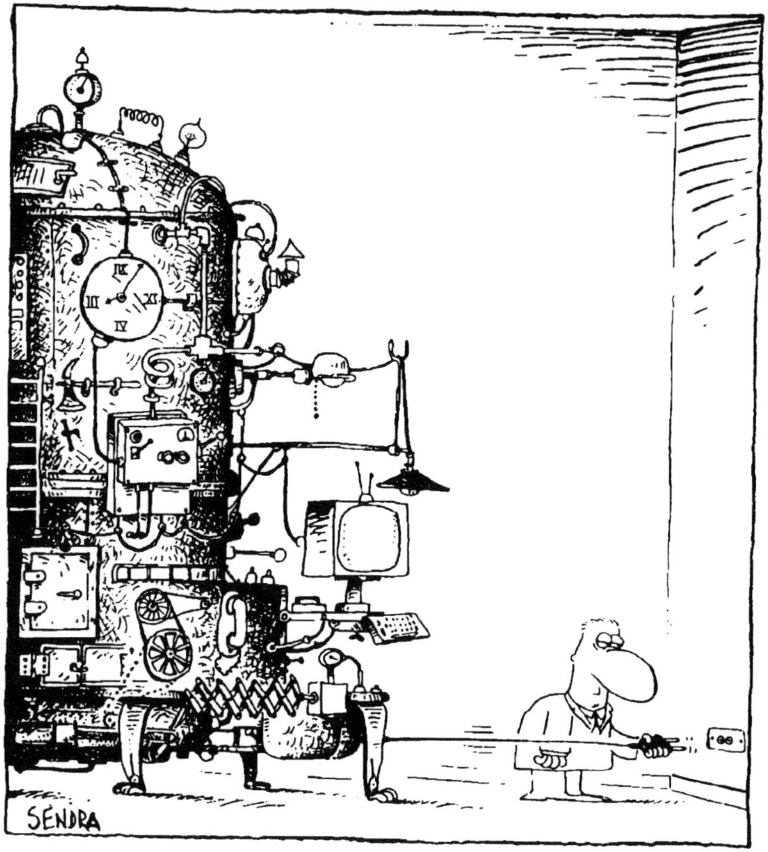
SENDRA

Image, Culture & Ecology

Culture

We can be knowledgeable with other men's knowledge,
but we cannot be wise with other men's wisdom.

~ Michel de Montaigne (1533-1592)

1. Rank the following human inventions according to the importance you think they have:

the wheel

writing   fire

nuclear energy

the microchip

the automobile

organ transplants

Image, Culture & Ecology

Culture

MORNING... CAN I TAKE UP A SHORT-TERM SEMINAR HERE?

YES, SIR

WHICH IS THE SHORTEST?

AN "INTRODUCTION TO CYBERNETICS"

OH, YOU MEAN "COMPUTERS"?

YOU'VE GOT THE RIGHT ANSWER! HERE'S YOUR DIPLOMA.

THANKS A LOT

©SENDRA

2. What do you think are the biggest differences between the following leaders?

George Washington   Attila the Hun
                      Napoleon
Alexander the Great   Julius Caesar

3. Which do you think is the oldest civilization still existing today?

4. Into how many historical periods would you divide the story of humanity?

5. Describe the contributions that the following people have made to civilization:

Homer   Einstein   Freud
          Marx   Neitzche
Voltaire   Confucious   Atahualpa
     Henry VIII   Tutankhamen
                Lao Tze

6. Put the following characters in their century and civilization:

Solomon   Goya   Paul
          Salgari   Ho Chi Minh
Copernicus   Benjamin Franklin   Machiavelli
     Hippocratus   Genghis Kahn

7. What is your understanding of Utopia? Describe it. Why do you think it is impossible to achieve?

8. How long ago do you think our species began on this earth?

9. What is the method for determining the age of very old material objects?

10. What is the primary theory that people use to account for the disappearance of the dinosaurs?

11. What is the main characteristic of the Peter Principle?

12. When did the first man land on the moon? Can you name the astronaut?

13. Which were the major military powers in the following centuries?

5th B.C.
       1st A.D.
              16th A.D.
                     20th A.D.

14. Name the date that the United Nations was founded.

15. What is Esperanto?

16. Who stated the following: "Truth makes us free"? How would you interpret this phrase?

17. Who stated the following: "There is no freedom without knowledge of our inner nature"? Socrates, Gurdjief, Rousseau, all of these people, none of these people.

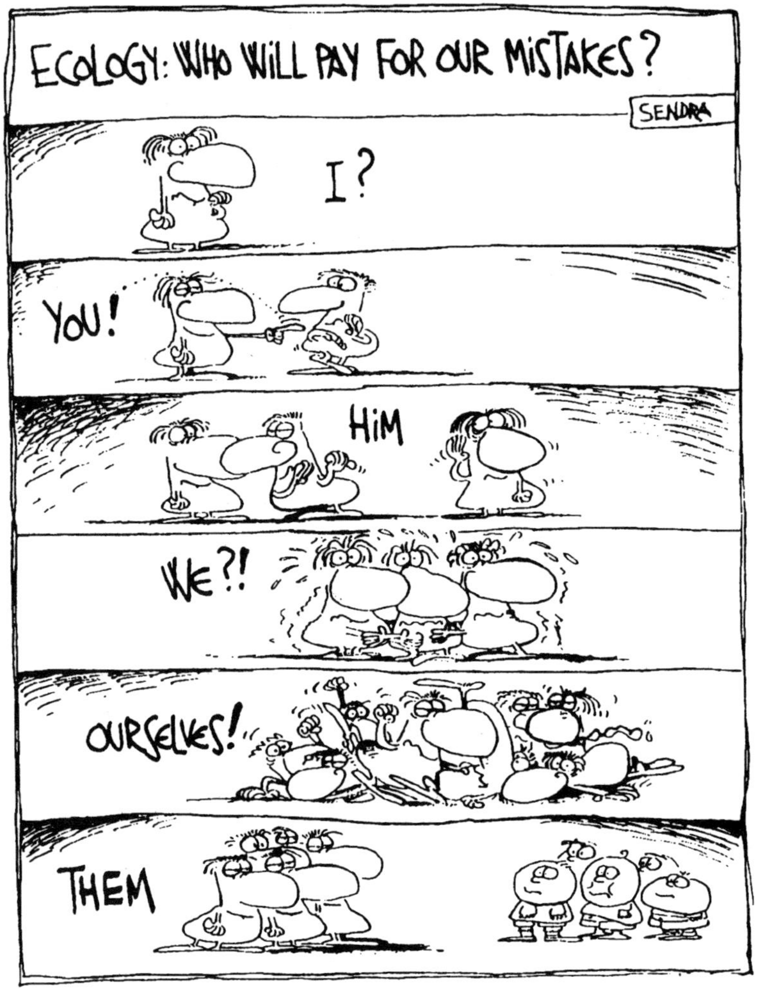
ECOLOGY: WHO WILL PAY FOR OUR MISTAKES?
SENDRA
I?
YOU!
HIM
WE?!
OURSELVES!
THEM

19 Image, Culture & Ecology

Ecology

The most important fact about Spaceship Earth:
an instruction book didn't come with it.

~ Buckminster Fuller

1. How many species have become extinct in the 20th century?

2. What are the major causes of the destruction of the ozone layer?

3. Do you think it is reasonable to be concerned about the extinction of our own species? Explain.

4. How good are our chances of surviving and developing over the next 5,000 years?

5. What do you think about the law of survival of the fittest?

6. Name the five main characteristics of people who will live 5,000 years from now. Do you think you will be like them? How do you think you will be different?

7. If your death could result in a useful benefit for mankind, what would you like the benefit to be? If your life could result in a benefit, what would you like it to be?

8. Do you think the overpopulation of the planet is real or fictitious?

9. How many inhabitants does your ideal city have? Which do you like better, the country or the city? Explain.

10. If an extraterrestrial could take you to a world where there was no pain and suffering, but you would never see anyone else on earth again, would you go?

11. Name your three strongest habits. What are the three habits to which you cling the most?

12. Imagine that our species created two new mutations. The first one is ten times more intelligent than we are, but also merciless, aggressive, and highly competitive. The second is only five times more intelligent, but also ten times more compassionate and loving. Which one would you choose to live? If these two species were to fight one another, which one would survive?

13. Which animal do you like the most? Describe the relationship between this animal and human beings.

14. Do you know what the "greenhouse effect" is doing to the planet?

15. To what degree, from 1-100, do you contribute to the pollution of our planet?

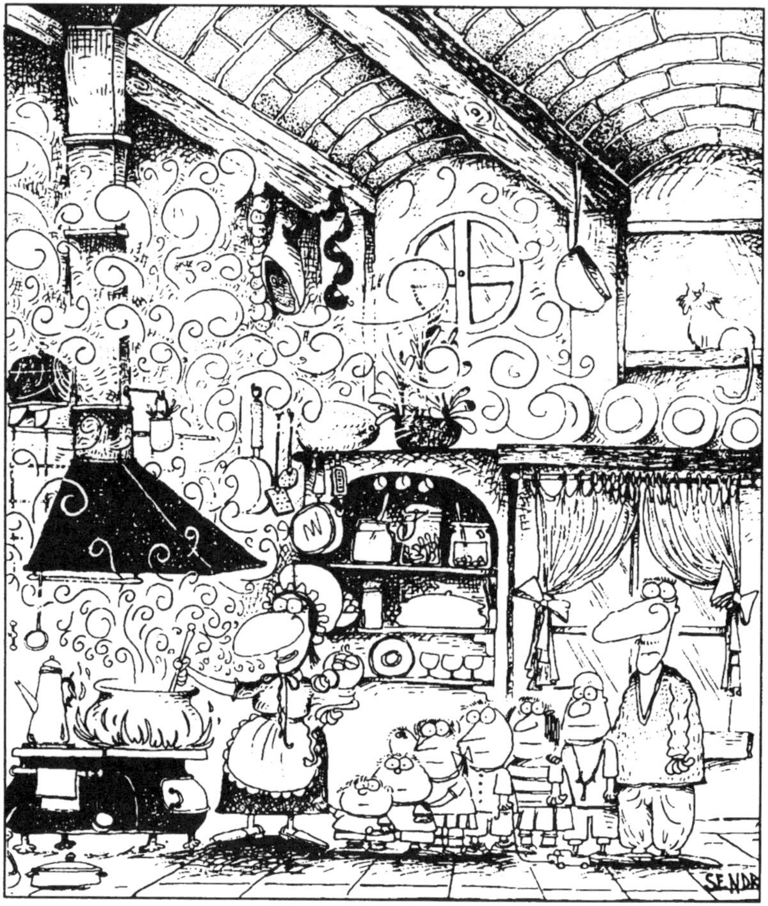
SENDA

20 History

General

If you want the present and the future to be different from the past, Spinoza tells us, study the past, find out the causes that made it what it was and bring different causes to bear.

~ Will and Ariel Durant

1. Do you consider yourself to be someone who is proud of your past, or would you prefer not to have a history? Explain.

2. What would you say are the five most important episodes in your life? Describe them.

3. In how many different cities or towns have you lived? What was the best or worst of each one?

4. Even if you haven't lived them, imagine and describe in one phrase, the following stages of your life:

infancy

        youth

                young adulthood

adolescence

           maturity

                old age

5. Who has been your best friend throughout your life? Describe his or her life.

6. Name the four most important characteristics you think each one of the following should have:

wife   *mother*   *father*

      son   *daughter*

friend   *husband*

7. What kind of life have you had? Describe it in one phrase. What kind of life did your father and mother have? Describe it in one phrase.

8. Which were the three main neuroses that your mother had when you were a child? Your father?

9. What is your oldest pleasant memory? What is your oldest unpleasant memory?

10. Were you a happy child? Explain.

11. How many brothers and sisters do you have? Where are you in the birth order? Describe your relationship with them.

12. Did your brothers and sisters love you? Did you love them?

13. Which one of them was/is your favorite?

14. Which one was/is your rival?

15. When you were a child, who was your best friend? Who was your worst enemy? How many friends did you have?

16. As a child, did you feel:
sad?   *frightened?*
     equal to other children?
healthy?   *sick?*
  different from other children?
superior?   *well-adapted?*
               alienated?
lonely?   *confident?*
               inferior?

17. Do you remember playing sexual games when you were a child? Describe the games. Do you now, or did you then feel guilty about these games?

18. Do you like your past? Rate it from 1-100, with 100 being idyllic.

19. What was your view of the world when you were a child?

20. Try to describe your first day at school. Describe three significant scenes from your first years at school.

21. Describe your first visit to the dentist.

22. Describe your first dance with a member of the opposite sex.

23. What is the one thing that you missed during your childhood?

24. What games did you play when alone? When you were with other children?

25. What did your neighbors think about your family?

26. What did your family think about your neighbors?

27. What sort of social status did your family have? Were they poor, rich, middle-class?

28. What ideas did your family have about money?

29. What did your family think about the big questions like God, Life, and the Universe?

30. What were the social and political ideas that your father had? Were they the same as your mother's ideas? Explain.

31. What ideas did you have about life when you were ten years old?

32. What did you think about sex when you were ten years old?

33. What did you want to be when you grew up?

34. Describe one important holiday that occurred during your childhood. What did you like to eat back then?

35. When you were twenty years old, how did you feel about: your family, yourself, society, your sexual life, your house, money and its availability to you, your future?

36. What are three major changes that you have experienced in the above categories since then?

37. How old are you now? What kind of person have you become?

38. What do you feel you owe your mother and father?

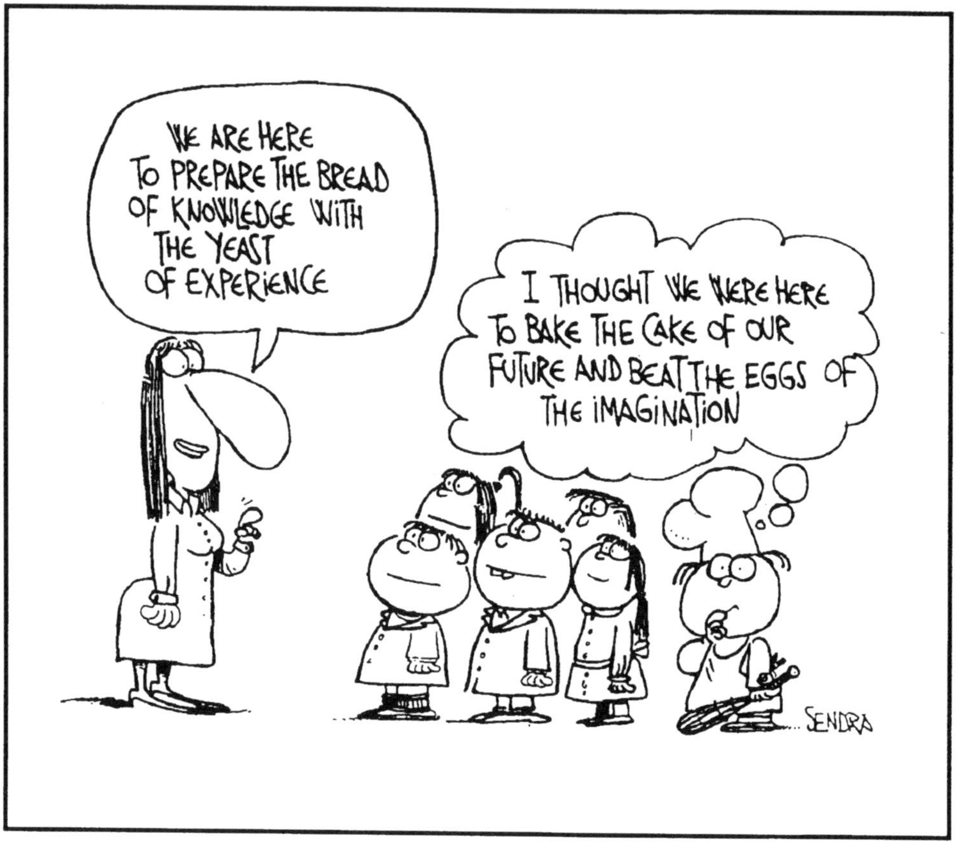
WE ARE HERE TO PREPARE THE BREAD OF KNOWLEDGE WITH THE YEAST OF EXPERIENCE
I THOUGHT WE WERE HERE TO BAKE THE CAKE OF OUR FUTURE AND BEAT THE EGGS OF THE IMAGINATION
SENDRA

21 History

Pre-History

The farther backward you can look, the farther forward you are likely to see.
~ *Winston Churchill*

Childhood decides.

~ *Jean Paul Sartre*

1. Briefly compare the approach to life between your two sets of grandparents. Fantasize out loud.

2. Do you imagine your birth was a happy and welcome event?

3. Were your parents hoping for a boy or a girl? If so, explain their preference.

4. How would you describe your mother's pregnancy? Happy? Difficult? Painful? What was society and her family like when your mother was pregnant? Fantasize about it.

5. How would you imagine the sexual act between your mother and father that resulted in your conception?

6. How was your birth for your mother? Was labor difficult? Easy? At home? In the hospital?

7. How was your birth for your father? Was he there? Was he nervous? Even if you're not sure, imagine and describe it.

8. What was your birth like? Imagine out loud.

9. Did your mother breast feed you? If so, for how long? What was her state of mind at the time? Fantasize and describe your feelings.

10. Imagine what it would have been like to see your mother and father flirting. Describe it.

11. What kind of girl do you think your mother was? What type of society and family was she raised in?

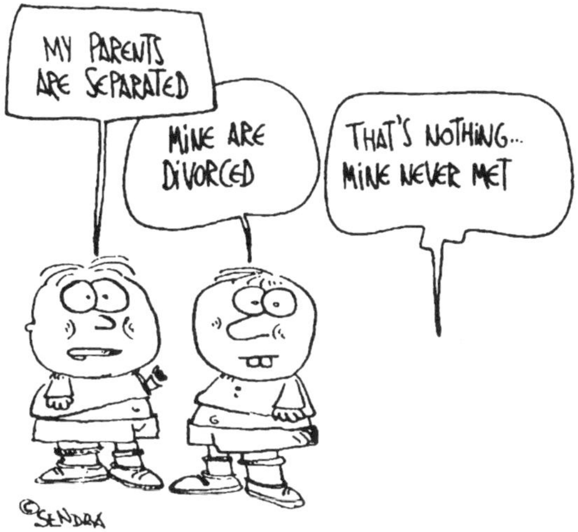

MY PARENTS ARE SEPARATED
MINE ARE DIVORCED
THAT'S NOTHING... MINE NEVER MET
©SENDRA

12. What kind of boy do you think your father was? What type of society and family was he raised in?

13. What were your mother's three worst and best traits in relation to your father?

14. What were your father's three worst and best traits in relation to your mother?

15. Think about what kept your parents together. Describe it.
love?
sex?
money?
status?
social pressure?
their parents?
ennui?

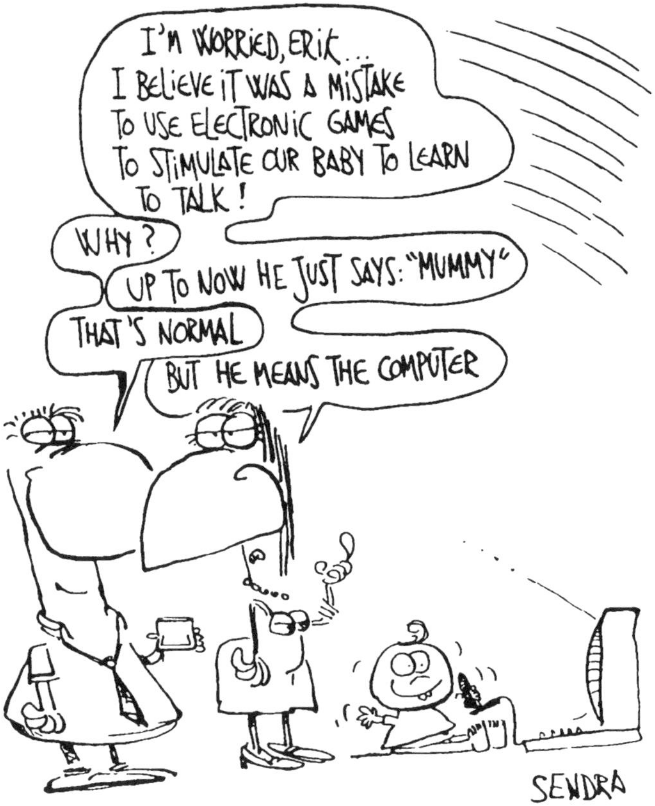
I'M WORRIED, ERIK... I BELIEVE IT WAS A MISTAKE TO USE ELECTRONIC GAMES TO STIMULATE OUR BABY TO LEARN TO TALK!
WHY?
UP TO NOW HE JUST SAYS: "MUMMY"
THAT'S NORMAL
BUT HE MEANS THE COMPUTER
SENDRA

16. Which of the following would describe the way your mother's family felt about your father?

he was loved

hated *rejected*

admired *respected*

ignored *feared* *envied*

Explain.

17. Which of the above discribes the way your father's family felt about your mother?

18. Who was your father's best friend?

19. Who do you think was your mother's best friend?

20. Imagine the social and historical circumstances of your four grandparents. Describe each grandparent with one phrase.

21. Imagine and describe an ancestor in your family that lived 600 years ago.

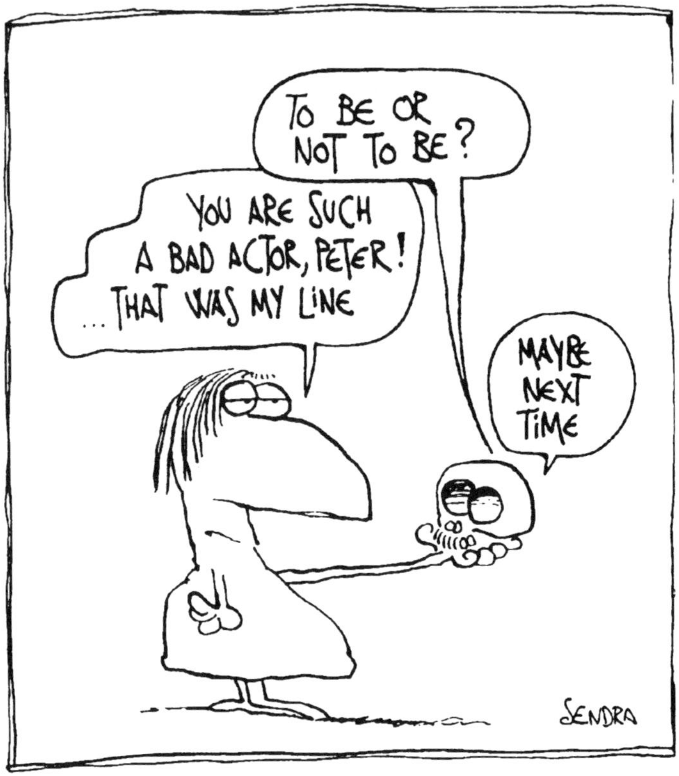

TO BE OR NOT TO BE?
YOU ARE SUCH A BAD ACTOR, PETER! ...THAT WAS MY LINE
MAYBE NEXT TIME
SENDRA

22 History

Meta-History

To know how to grow old is the masterwork of wisdom,
and is one of the most difficult chapters in the great art of living.
~ Henri Frederic Amiel (1821-1881)

1. At thirty years of age, what did you think, or what will you think, about the following?

your work

your family

your sex life

your potential

you fears

your future

your ambitions

your place in society

2. At forty-five years of age, what was, or what will be, your opinion about the following?

yourself

your father

your mother

your nuclear family

your economic situation

God and religion

your achievements

your future expectations

3. At sixty years of age, what was, or what will be your ideas about the following?

your life

love

society

your family

your achievements at this point in life

the rest of your life

4. What kind of life would you like to be living in 5, 10, 20, 30 years?

5. How many years do you expect to live?

6. What kind of friends do you want to have in ten years?

7. What is the best advice you have ever received?

8. Describe the best teacher you have ever had.

9. What is one of your lifelong dreams that you haven't fulfilled?

10. What was the happiest day of your life?

11. Quickly identify the major turning point in your life.

12. Are you still expecting some important changes in the unfolding of your life? What kind of changes are you expecting? Explain.

13. What would you like to leave the person you have loved the most if this person survives you?

14. Write your epitaph.

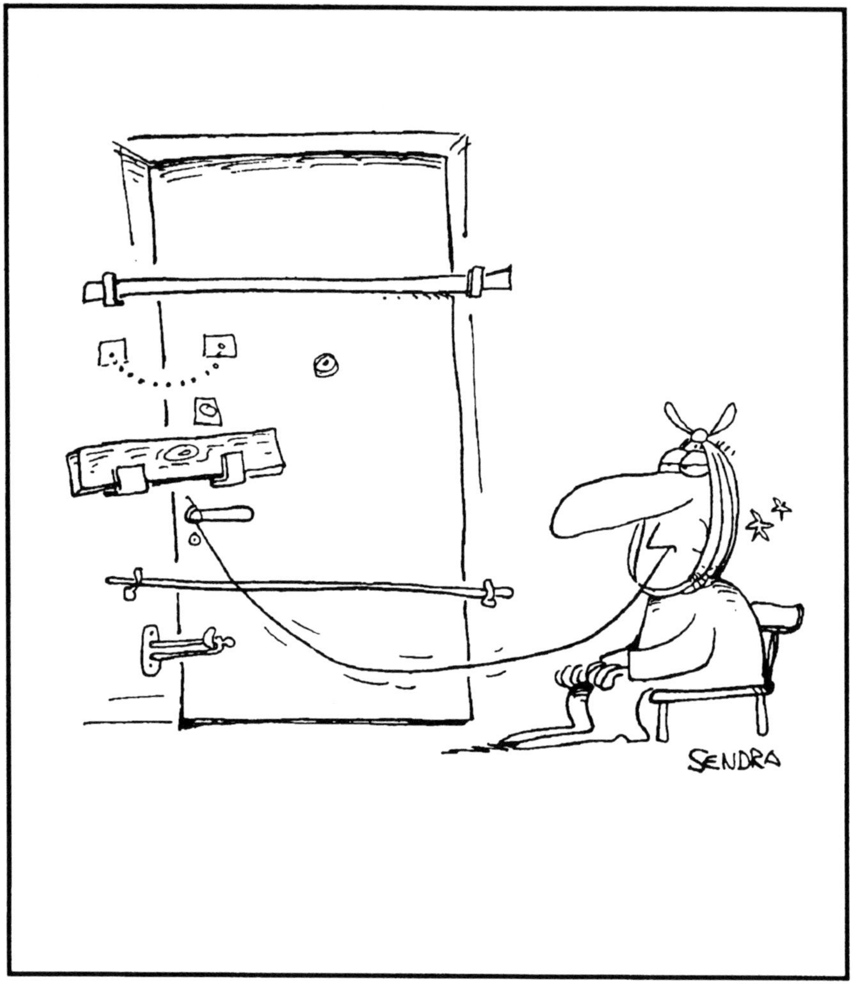
SENDRA

23 The Game of Truth

The ideas I stand for are not mine. I borrowed them from Socrates.
I swiped them from Chesterfield. I stole them from Jesus. And I put them in a book.
If you don't like their rules, whose would you use?
~ Dale Carnegie

1. What is a "relative truth" and an "absolute truth"? Name two, giving examples of them with situations that happened during the game.

2. Is truth dangerous? Is it better to lie? Under what circumstances? Which was the most false of your answers?

3. If this life is one of many reincarnations, do you think of your life as?
   a prize

   a punishment

   a random occurrence

The Game of Truth

4. Are you superstitious? If so, name 3 of your superstitions.

5. Name your three most controversial beliefs.

6. Assuming that heaven and hell do exist, if you were to die now, where would you go?

7. If you were born again, what in your life would you change?

8. Briefly describe the most exciting, playful and satisfying lovemaking experience that you have had.

9. Do you love someone more than yourself? If so, who? Who is the person you love most in this world?

10. What was your worst moment in this game?

11. Describe the most positive feeling you felt during the game.

12. What is the most interesting thing you have learned about yourself, if any, during this game? What is the most interesting thing you have learned about other players? Specify what and whom.

13. Rate from 1-100 the degree of truthfulness you have used during the game. Do you think you could play a rating of 100? Would you like it?

The Game of Truth

14. Of which player's judgement have you been most afraid? Why?

15. Define the three main characteristics of a group of friends.

16. Do you think that the acceptance and love of the other players for you has increased or decreased since the beginning of the game?

17. How do you feel about the players that have played with a low level of truthfulness?

18. Do you think that the love and comprehension of the group has increased or decreased since the beginning of the game?

19. Rate from 1-100 the degree of truthfulness and veracity of each one of the players.

Guideline for Giving Feedback

You're about to evaluate other people's answers to some challenging questions. You'll want to stay friends while offering useful feedback. You can share your observations without creating discomfort, intimidation or embarrassment.

First, frame your comments as "I" statements rather than "you" statements. The emphasis is on what you saw, observed, noticed. These comments invite introspection rather than a defensive posture.

Second, don't interpret! Leave analysis to the Player and/or his/her therapist. Let the Player explain or ponder.

Third, be specific and to the point. Long, meandering sentences that leave the Player wondering where you're going lack impact and effect and are easily forgettable. Provide direct, short bullets of observation for the most impact.

Finally, frame your observations in the positive. Speak to what you saw rather than what was missing!

Your feedback can be both useful and true!

RULES OF THE GAME

2-8 Players
(We recommend that children age 12+ play FAMILY selections, #1-9)

1. Choose a selection from 1-36.

2. The Reader reads Question 1 aloud.

3. Each player (rotating clockwise) answers each question (a Player may choose to pass twice).

4. Reader answers last.

5. Repeat for all 9 Questions

6. When all questions have been answered, each player (including Reader) assigns a Truthfulness number, 1-7 (with 7 highest) to all other players.

7. Total each player's score.

8. Winner is Player with highest score.

After some experience of the game, you may want to try Alternative Modes of Play (see next page) for variety, feedback and fun

Alternative Modes of Play

The Challenge Mode

1. If someone in the group challenges the truthfulness of an answer, that person may express his/her doubt by placing a token (a bean, coin, personal check, etc.) in "the pot".

2. Once the answer has been challenged, each player votes on the truthfulness of the answer. Majority rules. If the challenge succeeds, the Player matches the token in "the pot" and the challenger removes his/hers. If the challenge fails, the challenger's token remains in "the pot" to be distributed at the end of the game among all the Players.

The Truth on Trial Mode

This mode is a variation of the Challenge Mode. The challenger places no token but says, instead, "I want to put the truth on trial".

1. The group takes a vote and if a majority agree that the answer is untruthful, the challenger gains the right to ask 3 questions of his/her own design or may require that a certain task be performed by the Player (i.e., to sing, dance, recite, juggle, etc.).

2. If a majority consider the answer truthful, the Player who was doubted gets to ask three questions of the "doubter" or require him/her to perform a task.

Evaluation Mode

Negative									Positive	
Impatience, Irritability **ANGRY**	/								**SERENE**	Tollerance, Patience
Ambitious, Seductive **PROUD**				/					**HUMBLE**	Collaborative
image/prestige concern **VAIN**									**HONEST**	Authentic, Sincere
Gloom, Sadness **MELANCHOLIC**							/		**JOYFUL**	Cheer, Vitality
Closed, Stinginess **INTROVERTED**									**EXTROVERTED** Open, No-attachment	
Doubt, Distrust **FEARFUL**						///			**BRAVE**	Trust, Confidence
Attention-seeking, Planning **TALKATIVE**		/							**SOBER**	Temperate, Discreet
Excessive, Lustful **EXTREME**			//						**MODERATE** Innocent, Understanding	
Apathy, Sloth **INDOLENT**									**LOVING**	Sharing, Participation
Switch-off, Ignorant **TUNED-OUT**									**KNOWLEDGIBLE**	Clear, Objective
FALSEHOOD	////					///			**TRUTH**	
Evaluated by: *Annette*									Player: *Steve*	

When the game is completed, feedback can be shared by exchanging the cards (see "Guidelines for Giving Feedback" on page 133).

Evaluation Card Directions

It is suggested that this mode be played only after some experience of the game is garnered. This mode requires a committed group whose interest is in serious self-discovery and feedback. Choose your group wisely. You will need as many cards as there are Players. (Cards can be easily duplicated - pg. 138.)

Each Player will be evaluated on a separate card (include one for yourself). Fill in the names of the evaluator and the player on each card. The evaluation cards work on a double grid: FALSEHOOD-TRUTH and NEGATIVE-POSITIVE (see sample above).

While each Player is answering his/her question, the other players should bring their senses, feelings and judgment to bear on the answer being given. Ask yourself, "Is the Player telling the 'truth'? What are the vibes of the answer and his/her attitude towards the question?"

During the answer, or immediately after it, mark a tick on two of the grid lines. Mark the first along the FALSEHOOD-TRUTH continuum (how close to the Truth do you think the answer came?) and the second along the NEGATIVE - POSITIVE line the answer evokes. Which quality or personality defect are you perceiving as most intense in the Player? Is s/he afraid while answering? Then choose the FEARFUL-BRAVE line. Did the Player seem very patient, tolerant? Then choose the ANGRY-SERENE line. Each line offers 10 degrees of variation with the most excessive quality indicated by proximity to the DESCRIPTOR (ie. EXTREME-MODERATE). Ticks falling in between indicate degrees of moderation. By the end of the game, you will have 18 ticks dispersed among the lines (or condensed into fewer boxes, if appropriate).

At the conclusion of the game, share the cards. They indicate how you are perceived by others. Observe the concentration of your strengths and challenges, valuable and useful information. Give honest feedback. The quality and certainty of friendship rests in truthful sharing.

This mode can also be combined with the Challenge Mode. "The pot" is then given to the most truthful player!

Negative										Positive
Impatience, Irritability **ANGRY**										**SERENE** Tollerance, Patience
Ambitious, Seductive **PROUD**										**HUMBLE** Collaborative
image/prestige concern **VAIN**										**HONEST** Authentic, Sincere
Gloom, Sadness **MELANCHOLIC**										**JOYFUL** Cheer, Vitality
Closed, Stinginess **INTROVERTED**										**EXTROVERTED** Open, No-attachment
Doubt, Distrust **FEARFUL**										**BRAVE** Trust, Confidence
Attention-seeking, Planning **TALKATIVE**										**SOBER** Temperate, Discreet
Excessive, Lustful **EXTREME**										**MODERATE** Innocent, Understanding
Apathy, Sloth **INDOLENT**										**LOVING** Sharing, Participation
Switch-off, Ignorant **TUNED-OUT**										**KNOWLEDGIBLE** Clear, Objective
FALSEHOOD										**TRUTH**
Evaluated by:										**Player:**

Negative										Positive
Impatience, Irritability **ANGRY**										**SERENE** Tollerance, Patience
Ambitious, Seductive **PROUD**										**HUMBLE** Collaborative
Image/prestige concern **VAIN**										**HONEST** Authentic, Sincere
Gloom, Sadness **MELANCHOLIC**										**JOYFUL** Cheer, Vitality
Closed, Stinginess **INTROVERTED**										**EXTROVERTED** Open, No-attachment
Doubt, Distrust **FEARFUL**										**BRAVE** Trust, Confidence
Attention-seeking, Planning **TALKATIVE**										**SOBER** Temperate, Discreet
Excessive, Lustful **EXTREME**										**MODERATE** Innocent, Understanding
Apathy, Sloth **INDOLENT**										**LOVING** Sharing, Participation
Switch-off, Ignorant **TUNED-OUT**										**KNOWLEDGIBLE** Clear, Objective
FALSEHOOD										**TRUTH**
Evaluated by:										**Player:**

Self-Diagnosis Mode

This variation is for one Player. This is a healthy means of checking in with yourself.

Take some time and space for yourself, pen and paper in hand. Read the questions slowly, letting their full significance settle in your mind. Then answer reflectively and as truthfully as possible, moving on to the next question at a comfortable pace, without editing. When done, read over each question and your response… that in itself is excellent therapy.

Pg #-Qu.#	1-1	2-6	5-1	6-8	7-10	9-2
10-5	10-7	10-8	10-9	10-10	11-13	14-4
14-5	14-6	14-8	17-20	18-24	18-26	18-28
19-30	20-37	25-3	25-4	29-15	29-16	29-17
29-18	31-4	32-7	33-12	33-14	35-1	35-4
36-6	36-8	38-16	39-19	41-1	41-3	42-6
43-14	45-2	46-4	48-10	48-14	53-15	57-1
58-10	59-13+14	61-20	62-29	63-35	65-1	65-4
67-9	68-13	71-3	71-5	72-10	75-22	77-30
78-34	78-37	81-1	81-6	84-15	86-28	87-32
91-1	92-2	92-4	93-10	93-12	94-17	94-18
97-1	98-4	98-6	98-14	101-1	101-2	102-9
102-11	113-2	114-8	114-9	115-16	116-25	116-26
120-5	120-9	120-10	123-16	123-17	126-4	126-5
127-8	127-9	127-10	127-11	127-12	127-13	127-14
130-5	130-7	131-9	131-10			

FAMILY 1

1 Do you like your body? Describe it.

2 Name three of your personality traits that you like most.

3 What do you ask people close to you, to open up their hearts? Do you really offer this to them?

4 Of the people in the room, which one do you think is the most emotionally stable? And who is the most unstable?

5 Is it better to be a man or a woman? Why? Would you have preferred to be a different sex?

6 What are the three most important things in your life?

7 In your social environment, do you consider yourself: extraordinary, ordinary, different, unique, original, exclusive, chic, dirty, provocative, notorious, unknown or just one of the crowd?

8 What did you want to be when you grew up? If you are not an adult, what would you like to become?

9 What is the most interesting thing you have learned about yourself, if anything, during this game? What is the most interesting thing you have learned about other players? Specify what and whom.

FAMILY 2

1 What is your main goal in life?

2 How and when did you fall in love last? Describe it.

3 Of the people in the room, which one do you think will have fantasies of wild revenge for the things said about them today? Are you afraid of this possibility? If so, does this fear affect your answers?

4 Which member of your family knows you best? Which member of your family has the most distorted view of you?

5 Do you think you receive a fair amount of money for the work you do? If not, how much would be fair?

6 What is your worst habit?

7 If an extraterrestrial could take you to a world where there was no pain and suffering, but you would never see anyone else on earth again, would you go?

8 Do you have spare time? What do you do with it? Do you enjoy it? Why or why not?

9 Describe the most positive feeling you felt during the game.

1 Do you love your body? How much on a scale from 1 to 10?

2 If you could take any three people with you on a trip around the world, whom would you choose to take? If only one person?

3 Are you intelligent? On a scale from 1-10, where would you place yourself if 1 is imbecile and 10 is genius? Why? Explain.

4 Can you easily say what you feel about your family while you are in their presence?

5 What are the characteristics of the men and women (boys and girls) that you usually attract? Which characteristics are you usually attracted to?

6. What kind of work do you do? Do you like it? Why do you do it?

7 Do you think the overpopulation of the planet is real or fictitious? How do you feel in a crowd? Do you like groups or prefer being alone?

8 What is the best advice you have ever received?

9 Is truth dangerous? Is it better to lie? Under what circumstances? Which was the most deceitful of your answers?

1 When you are not with your friends, what do you think they say about you?

2 What is it that makes you happy and unhappy? Name two or three examples of each.

3 Are you affected by other people's opinion of you? Do you behave the same way with your family as with your friends?

4 Briefly describe the relationship between your mother and father.

5 If you were about to die, would you agree to a transplant of your heart, lungs, liver or pancreas?

6 Do you think animals have souls? Do they think? Do humans have souls? What does "soul" mean to you?

7 What is the image that other people have of you? Name your best friend and your worst enemy. Describe the image that each has of you.

8 Did your mother breast-feed you? If so, for how long? What was her state of mind at the time? Fantasize and describe your feelings.

9 Do you think that love and understanding in the group has increased or decreased since the beginning of the game? What would you suggest to increase this?

FAMILY 5

1 What thing or event has changed your life in the most dramatic way? Describe the situation. Explain your feelings.

2 In your opinion, what is the best talent that you possess? What talent do you wish most to possess?

3 Which person in the room do you think is probably a hypochondriac? And who is the most aggressive?

4 How do you feel about aging? Can you imagine yourself at 97? If so, describe your feelings.

5 Does money give you security? Do you feel depressed, unworthy or empty if you don't have money? Why?

6 If you were in a relationship and on one occasion your partner cheated on you, would you want to know?

7 Would you like to have more friends? If yes, what is preventing you from having them?

8 When you were a child, who was your best friend? Who was your worst enemy? How many friends did you have?

9 What is the most interesting thing you have learned about yourself, if anything, during this game? What is the most interesting thing you have learned about other players?

FAMILY 6

1 Name the three traits of your personality that you dislike most.

2 If you were going to die in a week, how would you spend it? If it were going to happen within 3 hours, whom would you like to speak to and why?

3 Would you name your child after yourself? Have you ever felt pride or shame in your first or last name? Have you ever thought of changing it? Have you?

4 When you were a child, what was the most frequent theme of conversation in your family? What was the subject spoken of least? Now that you are an adult, have the conversations changed? How have they changed?

5 What is "power" to you? How would you rank your actual degree of power if 1 is powerless and 10 is extremely powerful? Have you done something to change this? What kind of "power" do you use in your family relations?

6 Would you want your mate to be more attractive and intelligent than you ?

7 How many inhabitants live in your ideal city? Which do you like better, the country or the city? Explain.

8 If at your death, you knew that you could greatly benefit humanity by leaving your estate to a foundation, would you do it knowing that your family would then have to look after themselves?

9 Rate from 1-100 the degree of truthfulness of each one of the players.

1 Describe the last time you felt frustrated.

2 What are you usually doing while feeling you are wasting your time?

3 When was the last time you really yelled at somebody? Describe.

4 Have you ever thought about changing mates? Describe the situation. Did you do it?

5 If someone close to you had AIDS would you avoid that person? Would your answer change if that person were your brother or sister?

6 Describe your ideal family?

7 Of the people in the room, which one has a character most similar to your own? Describe the similarities.

8 What is one of your lifelong dreams that you haven't fulfilled?

9 Of which player's judgment have you been most afraid? Why?

1 If you could have anything in the world for your birthday, what would it be?

2 Name five people that know your truest feelings about things.

3 What would you change about the way you were raised? If you have children, have you tried to make those changes in the way you've raised them? How successful have you been in those improvements?

4 (M) Do you consider yourself a macho kind of man? Explain. (F) Do you consider yourself a feminist? Explain.

5 Would you like to be a more powerful man or woman? What is preventing you from having more power? Have you ever felt impotent?

6 What is your understanding of Utopia? Describe it. Do you think it is impossible to achieve? Explain.

7 What would you do if you heard that a good friend was criticizing you behind your back? Would you end the friendship? Would you confront the person? Or would you do the same - talk about this friend behind his/her back?

8 Would you consent to a series of genetic experiments that would result in many deformities if the experiments ultimately produced a superhuman? Explain.

9 If this life is one of many reincarnations, do you think of your life as: a prize, a punishment, a random occurrence? What achievement would make your life feel like a prize?

FAMILY 9

1 Have you ever thought about changing your physical appearance? What would you change? Describe the body that you would like to have.

2 If you were going to open a store and operate it yourself, what kind of store would it be? Describe it.

3. How and when did you fall in love last? Describe it.

4 In your opinion, what is the best talent that you possess? What talent do you wish most to possess? Have you ever felt envy of another person's talent? What was the talent? Do you cultivate your talents?

5 Name two famous people that you would have liked to have as parents. Would you like to have a life like theirs?

6 Of the people in the room, which one do you know the least about? Ask him/her a question.

7 If you saw someone drop $6,000 in old hundred dollar bills while getting into a new Rolls Royce and you got the license number of the car, would you make an effort to return the money?

8 Describe three religious figures that you admire. Why do you admire them?

9 What was your worst moment in this game? And what was your best feeling?

ADULT 10

1 What is death? What does it mean to you? What are your feelings about it?

2 If it could be done in total anonymity, which person in the room do you think would be most likely to sell themselves for money? Explain.

3 If you knew that your child was going to be born retarded and die at the age of five, would you accept an abortion?

4 If you were in a sinking ship and you could save either your mother or your father, but not both of them, which would you save?

5 What are the erotic points on your body? Name at least five.

6 Are you a moral person? Explain.

7 Who stated the following: "The Truth wil make us free"? How would you interpret this phrase?

8 What was your father's worst and best traits in relation to your mother?

9 Assuming that heaven and hell exist, if you were to die now, where would you go? During this game: What was the most hellish feeling for you? And your most heavenly moment, if any?

1 Have you ever examined your feet for a long period of time, looked at them carefully, and studied them? Remove your shoes and observe your feet for three minutes. As you do, express honestly how you feel about your physical being, yourself, and your love relationships.

2 Name three things in the world that you are the most thankful for.

3 Do you think it is possible to successfully lie to someone about your feelings? Have you ever done it? Explain.

4 Which person in the room has the most negative view of you as a person? Which one has the most positive view?

5 What is the worst thing you have done in order to gain more power?

6 Do your friends tell you honestly what they think about you? Or do they tend to tell you what you want to hear?

7 Do you think it is reasonable to be concerned about the extinction of our own species? Explain.

8 State briefly your opinion about the following: Yourself? The family you have constructed? Your economic situation? God and religion? Your personal achievements?

9 Define the three main characteristics of a group of friends.

ADULT 11

---

1 What is it that you like least about your body? Describe any particular eature, like scars, tattoos, or deformities. Are you overweight?

2 What are your 5 basic principles? Rate from 1-100 how you live according to them with 100 being "completely".

3 Have you ever done something that you felt was courageous? When? Describe what you did.

4 What would you do if one day you saw your mother being unfaithful to your father and on the next day your father came to you and told you what a wonderful, honest person your mother was?

5 What are the three best pieces of advice you would give to a child about sex?

6 What is friendship to you? Who is your best friend? What do you appreciate most in him/her?

7 What would you be willing to do for fame? Comment on the worst thing you have done in order to be noticed.

8 What is your oldest most pleasant memory? What is your oldest most unpleasant memory?

9 Do you believe telling the truth was a healthy experience for this group? What could you do or say to improve this feeling?

ADULT 12

ADULT 13

1 Is your body a source of suffering or of pleasure? Describe an event of intense suffering and another of great pleasure in your life.

2 What is your purpose in life?

3 Define the fundamental principle upon which your system of belief is based. What are your three main beliefs?

4 Are you able to accept help when you need it? How do you react to a situation of necessity or dependency?

5 Do you think some races are superior to others? If so, in what ways?

6 Do you think it is fair to pay taxes? If you can avoid paying taxes, do you do it?

7 What would you be willing to do for fame? Comment on the worst thing you have done in order to be noticed.

8 At seventy years of age, what would you like to think about the following: your life, love, society, your family, your achievements at this point in life, the rest of your life?

9 Rate from 1-100 the degree of truthfulness you have used during the game. Do you think you could play a rating of 100? Would you like it?

ADULT 14

1 Is your body: an object, a prison, a vehicle, an instrument, your destiny, or your being? Look at yourself in a mirror and improvise a poem or a few statements.

2 Which person in the room has the most distorted view of your personality? Why?

3 If you were going to die in a week, how would you spend it? If it were going to happen within 3 hours, whom would you like to speak to and why?

4. In your life, have you chosen to be like your parents or different from them? Explain.

5 Would you ever marry or have as a companion someone from another race or religion? Would your parents accept this?

6 If your best friend and your mother were drowning, whom would you save? Who is your best friend?

7 To what degree, from 1-100, do you contribute to the pollution of our planet?

8 What was the happiest day of your life?

9 Is truth dangerous? Is it better to lie? Under what circumstances? Which was the most deceitful of your answers?

1 What is required for you to be happy? On a scale from 1-100, with 100 being ecstasy, how would you rate your own happiness? Describe the most joyful scene you have ever lived.

2 When was the last time you were involved in a physical fight? Describe the circumstances and outcome.

3 If you were moving to another country and limited to three of your personal possessions, what would you take with you?

4 Since you were fourteen years old, what is the three-year period in which you have grown the most?

5 Do you consider yourself sexy? On a scale of 1-10, where would you place yourself if 1 is totally unattractive and 10 is a knockout?

6 Do you consider yourself friendly? How many real friends do you have? How long have these friendships lasted?

7 Describe the best teacher you have ever had.

8 What would you like to leave the person you have loved the most if this person survives you?

9 Do you love someone more than yourself? If so, who? Who is the person you love most in this world? Have you done anything to enhance your capacity to love?

ADULT 15

---

1 Name three things in the world that you are the most thankful for.

2 Describe your strongest bodily smells.

3 What is religion to you? How would you describe it? On a scale of 1-100, with 100 being extremely religious, how religious do you think you are?

4 Do you have homosexual friends? How do you feel about them? Do you have heterosexual friends? How do you feel about them? Do you feel 100% either?

5 Have you ever suffered for money? Explain why and when and describe the situation.

6 What do you think of people who are poor? What do you think of millionaires? Describe your interactions with each.

7 Name the two most important characteristics you think each one of the following should have: wife, mother, father, son, daughter, friend, and husband.

8 What were your mother's three worst and best traits in relation to your father?

9 Of which player's judgement have you been most afraid? Why? Invite him/her to ask you a question.

ADULT 16

ADULT 17

1 Have you ever thought about changing your physical appearance? What would you change? Describe the body that you would like to have.

2 Of the people in the room, which one do you consider the most extravagant? And who is the most "normal"?

3 Do you think it is possible to successfully lie to someone about your feelings? To yourself? Have you ever lied to yourself? Explain.

4 Do you trust your first impressions about people? When was the last time your first impression turned out to be wrong?

5 Mention three political figures you admire and tell why you admire them.

6 If you were engaged, would you cancel the engagement if an accident were to render your betrothed a paraplegic? If you were to became disabled?

7 What are the three habits to which you cling to the most?

8. Have you ever felt betrayed by a friendship? Describe the situation.

9 What is the most interesting thing you have learned about yourself, if any, during this game? What is the most interesting thing you have learned about other players? Specify what and whom.

ADULT 18

1 Describe the type of body you like in a partner. How is your partner similar or different to that type?

2 Would you prefer to give 20 million dollars anonymously to benefit many or to get $500,000 for yourself?

3 What is required for you to be happy? Name three conditions of happiness. Describe the most joyful scene you have ever lived.

4 Which person in the room do you know the least about? What would you like to know about him or her?

5 What are the three best pieces of advice you would give to a child about life? Do you practice them in your own life?

6 Would you start a relationship that would provide total satisfaction for one year knowing your partner would die a painless death at the end of the year? Would your answer be the same if your mate betrayed and left you instead of dying?

7 Do you think God knew Adam and Eve were going to sin? Why do you think God placed them in the garden?

8 In how many different cities or towns have you lived? What was the best or worst of each one?

9 Rate from 1-100 the degree of truthfulness you have used during the game. Do you think you could play a rating of 100? Would you like it?

1 What does death mean to you? Describe your feelings concerning the death of a beloved.

2 If you discovered an absolutely beautiful beach and then discovered that it was a nudist beach, would you leave or stay? If you'd stay, would you undress and walk around? Have you ever exhibited yourself? What were your feelings?

3 When you are worried, what percentage of your worries do you share with others? 5%, 15%, 30%, or? What is the biggest worry you have in your life right now?

4 Do you think you have had a more satisfying sexual life than your father and mother?

5 Have you lied for money? If so, describe the situation. Are you sure about your answer to the previous question? What about taxes, loans, self-image, etc.?

6 Have your intimate relationships changed since the AIDS virus became known? Explain. If a vaccine for the AIDS virus was invented, would you take it?

7. What kind of life have you had? Describe it in one phrase. What kind of life did your father and mother have? Describe it in one phrase.

8 What were your father's three worst and best traits in relation to your mother?

9. What was your worst moment in this game? And your most profound feeling of sympathy? With whom?

ADULT

19

---

1 If someone wrote a book about you, what would they title it? Would it be a comedy or a drama?

2 Are you satisfied with your sexual life? From 1 to 10 in what degree? Explain.

3 How do describe yourself to someone who doesn't know you?

4 What is the fundamental difference that distinguishes your 3 best friends? Name the friends and explain the differences.

5 In one sentence, state what the following people think about you: Mother, father, brothers and/or sisters, spouse, children.

6 If you had to choose between losing all your money or becoming either impotent or frigid, which would you choose?

7 Of the people in this room, which ones are capable of sneaking into a movie without paying? Have you done it?

8 Of the people in the room, who do you think is the most similar to you? Describe three similarities.

9 What is the most interesting thing you have learned about yourself, if any, during this game? What is the most interesting thing you have learned about other players? Specify what and whom.

ADULT

20

ADULT 21

1 Which member of your family knows you the best? Which member of your family has the most distorted view of you?

2 Are you part of a couple? if so: what degree of attunement do you have with her/him? (give a fast answer from 0 to 10): spiritual, intellectual, emotional, visceral, sexual, social convenience?

3 In your opinion, are some religions true and others false? How do you know?

4 On a scale of 1-10, with 1 being the lowest, at which level of the socio-economic scale are you? Can you do anything to change this? Have you tried to?

5 What do you think about artificial insemination? Would you adopt a child? How strong is your maternal or paternal instinct?

6 What is your understanding of Utopia? Describe it. Why do you think it is impossible to achieve?

7 What do you feel you owe your mother and father?

8 Name (at least 3) the qualities you look for in a friend. Do you possess these qualities?

9 Describe the most positive feeling you felt during the game.

ADULT 22

1 Do you like to dance? When was the last time you danced? Would you stand up and do a few dance steps?

2 Do you fart? Where and under what circumstances? Do you mind if somebody farts in front of you?

3 If you could choose to have either your body or only your brain age, which would you age?

4 As a child, did you feel: sad, frightened, equal to other children, different from other children, healthy, sick, superior, inferior, well-adapted, alienated, confident?

5 Do you feel any kind of shame or self-consciousness if you are answering sex-related questions? Why?

6 Describe the sexual behavior that satisfies you the most.

7 What kind of work do you do? Describe. Do you like it? Why do you do it?

8 When you are feeling really BAD, would you say you are: paranoid, depressed, hostile, or? Explain. Have you ever felt paranoid? Describe the situation.

9 Of the answers given by you today, which one gave you the most satisfaction?

1 In a week long period, how many days do you wake up tired or bored? In what season of the year do you feel best? Describe a perfect day.

2. What is it that makes you happy and unhappy? Name two or three examples of each.

3. How do you feel about aging? Can you imagine yourself at 97? Describe how you would like to be at that age and your mayor concern in becoming old. What is it that you fear?

4 To what degree does money bring you happiness? Rate the degree from 1-100, with 1 being none. How much money do you need for happiness?

5 What do your neighbors think about your family?

6 If you were given a magic wand that could do anything you could imagine, what three acts would you perform first?

7 With which person in the room would you be most willing to share your deepest, darkest secret? What is the secret?

8 In what ways do you consider yourself childish? Explain.

9 Give three words that best describe the way you are feeling right now. Do you think that the acceptance and love of the other players for you has increased or decreased since the beginning of the game?

ADULT 23

---

1 In a man, which part of the body do you look at first? In a woman, which part of the body do you look at first?

2 What are the three worst sins of your society?

3 What do you consider to be your three worst sins?

4 If you found out that your sexual partner were frustrated, would you mind if he or she experimented with others?

5 Name the person that believes your image of yourself is close to the truth? Which person believes your image is far from the truth?

6. Name the three main neuroses that your mother had when you were a child? Your father?

7 What is the thing you do best? What is the thing that gives you the most satisfaction?

8 If you were born again, what in your life would you change?

9. Briefly describe the most exciting, playful and satisfying lovemaking experience that you have had.

ADULT 24

ADULT 25

1 Have you ever had a problem with these internal organs: arteries, liver, stomach, bowels, kidneys, lungs, heart, or brain? Describe the problem.

2 Describe the moments of greatest solitude in your life.

3 When you are not with your friends, what do you think they say about you?

4 Have you ever loved another person for their money? Have you ever hated another person because of money? Explain.

5 What is your definition of success? Rate your success from 1-100.

6 What do you think about the law of survival of the fittest?

7 What was the happiest day of your life?

8 Name the three best things you have received from your family.

9 Rate from 1-100 the degree of truthfulness of each one of the players.

ADULT 26

1 How many more years do you think your body will live? How many more would you like to live? Do you think there is an ideal age to die?

2 Describe the conditions surrounding the last time you were depressed.

3 Of the people in the room, who do you think shares the least of their private life? Ask him/her a question.

4 What is it that you wanted most when you were a child? Did you acquire or achieve it?

5 (F) How are your menstrual periods? Are they regular? (M) Do you ever have trouble getting on erection? Explain.

6 Think about what kept your parents together, love, sex, money, status, social pressure, their parents? Explain.

7 Would you accept living as a "bionic man"?(Artificial high efficiency limbs and internal organs with your own face and brain)

8 Do you accept the concept of euthanasia? Would you perform euthanasia on your father or mother? And if they had previously asked for it?

9 What is the most interesting thing you have learned about yourself, if any, during this game? What is the most interesting thing you have learned about other players? Specify what and whom.

1 Do you have a special room in your house? If so, describe it. If not, why not? Describe that special place you feel essentially yours.
2 What is your relationship with your neighbors?
3 Do you make sure that you always thank the people who help you? Describe a situation where you experienced deep and real gratitude
4 Have you or would you cheat on a test? Have you lied for money, for love, for acceptance? Describe.
5 When was the last time you felt embarrassed? Describe the situation.
6 Even if you're not sure, imagine and describe, how your birth was for your father?
7 What is the most important thing a friend has ever given you? Describe the relationship with your very best friend.
8 If you knew that you were going to die in one year, what would you change about your life? Write your epitaph.
9 Rate from 1-100 the degree of truthfulness of each one of the players.

ADULT 27

1 Which one of the following describes you best: follow the religion of my parents; rebel against the religion of my father or family; converted to another religion; or don't believe in or belong to any religion?
2 Do you believe in the existence of a spirit that continues to live after you die? If so, on what do you base this belief?
3 In one sentence, state what the following people think about you: Mother, father, brothers and/or sisters, spouse, and children, your best friend.
4 If you discovered that you were going to reincarnate as an animal and could choose, which animal would you become? Which animal would you least like to become? Explain.
5 Which of the following is preferable: celibacy, to masturbate alone, to be part of a couple in total fidelity, short term couple, occasional sexual partners, group sex?
6 Do you remember playing sexual games when you were a child? Describe the games. Do you now, or did you then feel guilty about these games?
7 What is one of your lifelong dreams that you haven't fulfilled?
8 Of which player's judgement have you been most afraid?
9 What are the three things that you want to be remembered for? Why?

ADULT 28

ADULT 29

1 If you could have chosen the family into which you were born, what would it be like? Describe it. In what way does this diverge from you real family?

2 Do you vote in elections? If so, what party do you vote for? Why?

3 If you were going to go into therapy, which type would you choose?
Faith Healing, Jungian, Freudian, New Age Short Therapies, Gestalt, Primal Scream, or a nice chat?

4 Do you think it is better not to talk about sex? Why or why not? What do you think would be a daring sexual question? Answer it.

5 Have you ever killed a living creature? A fly, a mouse, a cat, a bird, or a human being? If so, describe how you killed it and how you felt.

6 Of the people in the room, which one do you think accepts a mistake the easiest? And who finds it hardest to accept a mistake?

7 Describe your immediate society and explain your role in it.

8 Have you ever-used external imaginary stimulation during sex: videos, imagining a different partner, etc.?

9 What would you like to do to make someone in this group feel better?

ADULT 30

1 What are the three most important things in your life?

2 Does your sexual partner verbalize his or her sexual desires? If yes, do you enjoy it? If no, do you wish s/he would?

3 Would you mind if your mate or sexual partner had sex with someone else if it were part of a therapeutic sexual program?

4 How much money would it take for you to play a round of Russian roulette? Would you take that risk to save someone's life? Who's?

5 What opinion did your mother's family have of your father?

6 Of the people in the room, which one do you think has the most interesting fantasy life? Fantasize for a moment and describe it.

7 Describe the sexual behaviors that you practice the most.

8 Of the people in this room which one do you think makes the best friend? And who's the most confrontational as a friend?

9 What was your worst moment in this game? And your most positive feeling?

1 Who is the most assertive person in the room? And who is the least assertive?

2 When was the last time you had a family conflict about finances? Describe.

3 What is the most unpleasant thing you have ever done for money?

4 If you could choose the way that you were going to die, but doing so meant that you would live one year less, would you opt to choose? What would be your preferred way to die?

5 If by sacrificing 35% of your current intellectual ability you could extend your life by 30 years, would you do it? How much of your intelligence would you give up in order to live longer?

6 What do you think of prostitution? Have you ever had sex with a prostitute?

7 Would you subject yourself to an experiment that might leave you permanently disabled or deformed if it resulted in a lot of money for your family and progress for humanity?

8 If someone in your immediate family were suffering from mental illness, would you have them live with you and share your life? Or would you put them in an institution? Would the answer be different if you knew there was no cure?

9 Are you honest? On a scale from 1-10 where would you place yourself if 1 is thoroughly dishonest?

ADULT

31

---

1 Who do you consider to be lucky? Guess who is the most lucky person in the room. Why?

2 Have you ever thought about suicide? Have you ever attempted it? What were the circumstances?

3 Are you able to verbalize your sexual desires? Describe one.

4 What amount of money would you steal if you were sure of not being caught?

5 If you knew that you were going to die in six months, would you be willing to be frozen now for 1,000 years in order to have a 15% possibility of being cured when awakened? Would you do it if there were a 50% chance?

6 On a scale of 1-10, with 1 being total rejection and 10 being complete loyalty, rate your respect for traditional values.

7 What do you think about abortion? Are there any conditions where you would accept it? Have you practiced it? If so, what were your circumstances and feelings?

8 Describe your relationship with your brothers and sisters.

9 If you were to die tonight, is there anything you would regret not having said? What? To whom?

ADULT

ADULT 33

1 Do your friends tell you honestly what they think about you? Or do they tend to tell you what you want to hear?

2 What would you do if you found $5,000 in bills on the street? Would you spend it? On what?

3 At what age do you think you will stop having sex? When did you last have intercourse and how much, on a scale of 1 to 10, did you enjoy it?

4 Rank the people in the room from the most intelligent to the least.

5 Would you begin a relationship that would give you total satisfaction for one year if you knew at the start that your mate would die (with no pain) at the end of the year? Would you begin a relationship that would give you total satisfaction for one year if you knew at the start that your mate would betray you at the end of the year?

6 Would you kill another human being because of your faith?

7 What is the worst thing a parent can do to his/her children? Was this done to you as a child? Have you ever done it to your children or to any other child?

8 Would you donate a kidney (while alive) to your mother, father, mate, brother, sister, child, or best friend? Do you give blood?

9 Where do you make friends? Work, neighborhood, school, family, church, hobbies, or political groups? Who could be your best friend in this group?

ADULT 34

1 What is the best advice you have ever received?

2 Would you like to have a clone brother or sister, (genetically identical with you)? Look at a mirror and fantasize that your image comes alive: What would that relation be? Do you love yourself? What is it that you most hate in yourself?

3 What is your worst habit? Explain.

4 What is your most obsessive thought? Explain.

5 If you could travel trough time in a time-machine, go to your past and change something of your personal or family past, what would you change?

6 Have you ever used psychedelic drugs? Antidepressants, tranquilizers? Describe.

7 What is your primary motive for having sex? Reproduction, pleasure, instinct, communication, or mystical union? Are you really satisfied with your sexual life? How much on a scale 1 to 10?

8 In this group, who do you think can best play a mother's role? And a father's role? Explain.

9 Do you love someone more than yourself? If so, who? Who is the person you love most in this world?

1 Describe yourself in only one word. If you could live the life of any historical figure in human history who would you like to be?

2 How would you like to spend the last day of your life? With whom? Doing what?

3 Would you accept $10,000,000 in cash to leave your country, family and friends for 20 years? Would you work as a slave for 10 years to get that amount?

4 Describe the ideal mother and father. In what way does this differ from your real parents?

5 Have you ever lied to yourself? What was your worst self-deceit?

6 Have you tried "Viagra" or other sexual stimulants? Would you like to do so? Have you been impotent or frigid in any period of your life?. Describe.

7 Describe each person in this group with an epithet, nickname or Indian-name (a name that characterizes and caricatures).

8 Who was your father's best friend? Have you improved on your father's ability for friendship? Can you do something to improve?

9 Are you still expecting some important changes in the unfolding of your life? What kind of changes are you expecting? Explain.

ADULT 35

---

1 When you are worried, what percentage of your worries do you share with others? 5%, 15%, 30%, or? What is the biggest worry you have in your life right now?

2 What is you main purpose in life? What degree of achievement have you got?

3 Name some of the things you consider to be sexual perversions. Of these, how many have you practiced? Have you ever fantasized about any of these perversions?

4 What does "power" means to you? How powerful or powerless do you feel in life? What is the worst thing you have done in order to gain more power?

5 Do you drink alcohol? Does it change your personality, feelings and behavior? Do you smoke tobacco? Do you consider this a drug addiction? Have you made use of other drugs?

6 Would you give your life to save that of another human being? Your parents, your children, your husband or wife, your brother or sister, your best friends? To save your country?

7 How proud are you of the life you are living? What in your life is it that makes you especially proud?

8 What is the best advice you can give to each person in this group?

9 What does friendship means to you? Who could be your best friend in this group?

ADULT 36